Glenelg Country School

John F. KENNEDY

John F.

KENNEDY

YOUNG PEOPLE'S
◇PRESIDENT◇

CATHERINE CORLEY ANDERSON

LERNER PUBLICATIONS COMPANY · MINNEAPOLIS

Front cover photograph courtesy of the Minnesota Democratic-
Farmer-Labor Party Central Committee
Back cover photograph courtesy of the John F. Kennedy Library

Library of Congress Cataloging-in-Publication Data

Anderson, Catherine Corley.
    John F. Kennedy / Catherine Corley Anderson.
       p.   cm.
    Summary: Describes the vibrant and witty thirty-fifth president of
the United States.
    Includes bibliographical references.
    ISBN 0-8225-4904-2
    1. Kennedy, John F. (John Fitzgerald), 1917-1963—Juvenile
literature. 2. Presidents—United States—Biography—Juvenile
literature. 3. United States—Politics and government—1961-1963—
Juvenile literature. I. Title.
    [DNLM: 1. Kennedy, John F. (John Fitzgerald), 1917-1963.
2. Presidents.]
F842.Z9A63   1990
973.922'092—dc20
[B]
[92]   90-6158
                                                         CIP
                                                         AC

Manufactured in the United States of America

1 2 3 4 5 6 7 8 9 10 00 99 98 97 96 95 94 93 92 91

Contents

Acknowledgments

I wish to acknowledge with gratitude the many people who graciously added to my information and understanding of John F. Kennedy. Among them are: David Powers, special assistant to the president; William Johnson, crew member, PT 109; William Mokray, former vice president, Boston Celtics; Rev. George H. Dunne, S.J., Director, Peace Corps Training, Georgetown University; Professor Emeritus Arthur Holcombe, Department of Science of Government, Harvard University; Mary Hibbard, teacher, Conniston School, West Palm Beach, Florida; E.B. White, author and recipient of the Freedom Award; Peace Corps volunteer Judy Smith; Kathleen Ann Corley; Pamela Higgins, Patrick McFarland, Debbie Wulf, David Johnson, Betsy D'Angio, Jim Kramer.

The photographs and illustrations in this book are reproduced through the courtesy of: the Department of the Army, p. 50; Independent Picture Service, pp. 2, 99; John F. Kennedy Library, pp. 8, 12, 13, 18, 21, 22, 26 (top), 31 , 35 (both), 37, 38, 44 (both), 47 (both), 48, 49, 54 (bottom), 57, 58, 63 (bottom), 66, 68, 75, 76, 79 (both), 93, 94 (both), 98, 101, 102 (bottom), 106, 108, 109 (both), 110 (both), 112 (both), 115 (bottom), 116, 118, 122, 123, 127 (both), 130, 131 (bottom), 132, 133, 134, 136, back cover; Library of Congress, p. 41; Minnesota Democratic-Farmer-Labor Party Central Committee, pp. 1, 54 (top), 89,124, front cover; Minnesota Historical Society, p. 63 (top); National Archives, p. 92 (bottom); National Aeronautics and Space Administration, p. 115 (top); Peace Corps, pp. 80, 83; Schomburg Center for Research in Black Culture, p. 86; Southdale-Hennepin Area Library, pp. 70, 128; United Nations, p. 56; U.S. Navy, p. 26 (bottom); University of Mississippi, p. 87; UPI, pp. 92 (top), 131, 135; Laura Westlund, p. 32 (map).

Dedication

This book is dedicated to the memory of my dear departed parents, Gaynor J. and Anna Higgins Corley, who gave me such a happy childhood, and to my dear husband, Mel Anderson, who was always my right-hand man.

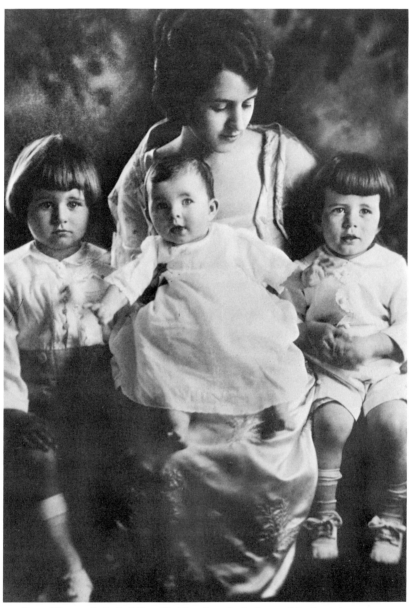

Rose Kennedy is holding Bobby. Joe, Jr., left, *and Jack,* right, *are beside her.*

◊ ONE ◊

Growing up Rich

1917-1938

The boys and girls of West Palm Beach, Florida, often caught glimpses of President John Kennedy driving his white convertible down Southern Boulevard or piloting a boat on Lake Worth. The president's parents, Rose and Joseph Kennedy, had a home there, and the president often flew down for a weekend visit.

Conniston Junior High School students were among those who waved at him as he passed by. In a "People to People" program at school, they had chosen a school in Florina, Greece, as a partner. The students wanted to make a film showing their life in the United States—their homes, their school, their churches, different parts of their city, and their public officials. The governor of Florida, the mayor of the city, and the police and fire chiefs had all agreed to take part. Did they dare ask the president to join them?

With Mrs. Hibbard, their teacher, to spur them on, they dared. They wrote to the president, asking him if, on his Easter visit, he would permit them to take his picture.

They waited anxiously for a reply. When it came, there were groans of disappointment. The answer had not come directly from the president. It was signed by one of his aides, who said he was sorry but the president would not be able to help them.

That was that, they thought. But one day a student's mother looked out of the window of the camera shop where she worked and saw John Kennedy parked in his car. She rushed out and approached the president.

"May I impose on you, Mr. President?" she asked.

John Kennedy flashed his famous grin and answered, "Go ahead. Impose."

She explained the students' plans. Could the president possibly help them?

It was plain that this was the first time John Kennedy had heard of Conniston Junior High's project. He looked interested.

"I'd like to help," he said. Then he explained that he was leaving for the airport soon to return to Washington. Would it be possible to get the boys and girls and their film equipment to the airport in an hour? The president would see that they were passed through the guards.

The Conniston mother went into action. So did President Kennedy. Within the hour fourteen 12-year-olds and four adults passed through the Secret Service guards at the airport. The young cameraman, who was president of the student council, made a short speech. He explained the purpose of their project. When he had finished, the president said —not wholly in fun— "I'm glad to know that the job of keeping international peace is not left entirely up to my administration."

The president shook hands with all the young people and adults, spoke to them, and posed for pictures. The camera was still rolling as he climbed the ramp to the plane. He turned and waved before entering the plane. Afterward the mother who had arranged the Democratic president's appearance exclaimed, "I just can't get over his kindness in doing it—and I'm a Republican!"

John Fitzgerald Kennedy, the 35th president of the United States, was born on May 29, 1917, in a big frame house at 83 Beals Street in Brookline, Massachusetts. It was a pleasant, three-story house with a wide front porch and white pillars. A fireplace was in the living room—and a piano, which had been given to Rose Kennedy by an uncle.

Young Jack, as John soon was called, had scarlet fever when he was four years old. He also had several other childhood diseases. Perhaps this was why he was small for his age. His older brother, Joe, was much bigger and stronger. Joe took it upon himself to be Jack's coach and protector.

Secretly Jack admired his big brother, but it bothered him sometimes to have Joe always telling him what to do. Jack could never be as good as Joe in sports, but he tried awfully hard.

Life was full of fun and activity in the house on Beals Street. The boys soon had younger sisters. Rosemary was born in 1918, Kathleen came a little more than a year later, and Eunice followed in 1921. In the winter, their father, Joe Kennedy, Sr., took his children for rides on a homemade sled. In the summer, Grandpa Fitzgerald took them to watch the Boston Red Sox, his favorite team, play baseball.

Rose Kennedy often planned family trips to historic places around Boston. The young Kennedys loved to visit Boston Harbor. Their mother told them the thrilling story of the Boston Tea Party. Both parents impressed on their children that their country had been good to the Kennedys. Whatever benefits the family received *from* the country, they were told, must be returned by performing some service *for* the country.

Jack's father was a very successful businessman, and he became quite prosperous. In 1926 the family moved to Riverdale, New York. Jack spent his grammar-school days at Riverdale Country Day School in West Bronx, New York. Jack was just an average student. His sixth-grade teacher, Miss Irene Guiney, said he was chiefly noted for his sense of humor and for his desire to excel—mostly in sports. He liked

Both Jack (first row, second from right) *and Joe, Jr.,* (second row, fourth from left) *were on the Dexter School football team in Brookline, Massachusetts.*

The Kennedy family, from left to right: *Bobby, Jack, Eunice, Jean, Joe, Sr., Rose, Pat, Kathleen, Joe, Jr., Rosemary*

history and English, but he was a very poor speller and not very good in science or math.

Jack was still small and slight for his age. He had widely spaced eyes, freckles on a tipped nose, and large front teeth. His thick, unruly hair tumbled over his forehead.

At 13 Jack went away to school for the first time. He attended Canterbury School, a boarding school in New Milford, Connecticut. Jack was pretty homesick the first month. He wrote home to ask for golf balls, a "puff quilt" (his description of a down-filled comforter), and chocolate cream pie. He also asked for 35 cents more a week in his allowance to pay his Boy Scout dues, and "to pay my way around."

The family had grown to include Patricia, Bobby, Jean, and Edward, who was called Ted or Teddy. Rose Kennedy now had servants to help with the housework, so she could spend more time with her busy, noisy family. Joe Kennedy bought homes in West Palm Beach, Florida, and Hyannis Port, Massachusetts.

It was at Hyannis Port that Jack acquired his love for the sea and learned how to handle small boats. He named his first sailboat *Victura,* which meant "something about winning," he said. This was in keeping with the Kennedy code, instilled in the children by their father. They were taught that one must always try to be first, to be the best.

At Easter Jack had an attack of appendicitis and was rushed to the hospital. He couldn't finish the spring term at Canterbury. The next fall, 1931, he enrolled at Choate Preparatory in Wallingford, Connecticut. His older brother, Joe, had been there for a year. Joe was on the football, baseball, and hockey teams, and he was very good in his studies.

Jack quickly formed his own circle of friends. Lemoyne (Les) Billings and Ralph (Rip) Horton were his buddies. With half a dozen other boys they started a club called the "Muckers." The members often got into trouble. Although students were not allowed to leave the school grounds without permission, one night the Muckers sneaked out to the local ice cream parlor after hours. On their way back to their rooms, they ran smack into the headmaster!

The boys were in danger of being expelled, and their parents were notified. When Joe Kennedy arrived at the school, Jack confessed his part in the "monkey business." He promised his father he would put more effort into his studies. All the boys were given a second chance.

He was 18 when he graduated from Choate in 1934. He had grown tall, lanky, and good-looking, but his snub nose and unruly hair made him look much younger than his age. He often wished he were as handsome and polished as his brother Joe.

Jack had been promised a trip to London as a graduation gift. His father wanted him to attend a summer session at the London School of Economics, but Jack protested. He thought the trip was to be a holiday, and that Professor Harold Laski, who ran the school, was supposed to be a Communist.

Mr. Kennedy said that he didn't expect Jack to agree with the professor's beliefs, but that it was a good idea to learn other points of view besides his own. Jack didn't get much chance to put his view into practice. He had hardly started class when he became ill. He felt weak and his skin turned yellow. A doctor told him he had jaundice and would have to go to the hospital.

As soon as he was allowed to travel, Jack left for Hyannis Port. He spent the rest of the summer trying to recover. He wasn't entirely well when he started Princeton, several weeks late, in the fall of 1935.

Jack entered Princeton to find his friends, Les and Rip, settled in a shabby, fourth-floor room in South Reunion Hall. The furniture was moth-eaten and the bathroom was in the basement, but Jack was just happy to be with his friends.

He was still weak and tired. The doctor had ordered no athletics, so he was limited to being only a spectator. His friend Rip was a wrestler and boxer, so Jack contented himself with being Rip's trainer and manager.

Around Christmas the jaundice recurred, and Jack had to drop out of school. His doctor prescribed rest in a warm climate. Jack went to Arizona, soaked up the sun, and read all the books he could lay his hands on. Before the next school year began, he told his father he wanted to go to Harvard.

These were exciting times at school and around the world. On campuses, young people took a keen interest in politics, social changes, and events in Europe. The United

States was pulling out of the Great Depression, which had gripped the country in the '30s. The depression had begun in 1929 with the collapse of the stock market and the widespread failure of banks and businesses. Bread lines and soup kitchens—where hungry people stood in line for handouts of food—had become a common sight. One out of four workers was unemployed. Thousands of people had joined a "hunger march" on Washington, demanding jobs so they could feed their families.

Joe Kennedy's insight and shrewd maneuvers had saved him from financial disaster. He bought stocks at a very low price and held them until their value increased. Then, at just the right moment, he sold them and made a large profit.

It was at this time that Jack first became aware of the vast social and economic differences in the United States. The fellows at school talked about such things, and Jack, a rich man's son, came in for some good-natured kidding. But Jack cared about poor people and wondered what he could do to help them.

Joseph Kennedy had supported Franklin Delano Roosevelt when he ran for president in 1932. Roosevelt won the election. When he became president, Roosevelt started many programs to help the unemployed and to get the economy back to normal. In an effort to prevent the careless and dishonest business practices that contributed to the collapse of the economy in 1929, Congress created the Securities and Exchange Commission to set up regulations for the stock market. In return for Kennedy's support during the presidential campaign, Roosevelt appointed him chair of the new commission.

President Roosevelt was also watching events in Europe, as Hitler's Nazi Germany followed a policy of aggressive territorial expansion. In 1937 President Roosevelt appointed Joseph Kennedy the United States ambassador to Great Britain. It was an important position, and the appointment made Mr. Kennedy very happy. Joe, Jr., and Jack stayed at Harvard, but the rest of the family moved to England. The English were charmed by the handsome Kennedys, and the Kennedys enjoyed living in London. Mr. and Mrs. Kennedy were even invited to spend a weekend visiting with the king and queen at Windsor Castle.

Meanwhile, Europe was teetering on the edge of war. Ambassador Kennedy kept President Roosevelt informed about events taking place. In September 1938, Prime Minister Neville Chamberlain of England met with the German dictator, Adolf Hitler, in Munich, Germany. In an attempt to stop Hitler's expansion and avoid war, Chamberlain agreed to allow the Germans to take over a part of Czechoslovakia. In return, Hitler promised that that would be his last territorial claim.

Within a few months, however, Hitler broke his promise and took control of all Czechoslovakia. Soon afterward he attacked Poland. Since England and France had pledged to defend Poland, they declared war on Germany. On September 1, 1939, World War II began. Ambassador Kennedy advised Roosevelt that the United States should not become involved in what he considered a European war.

Jack visits with a woman in Belgium in 1939.

◊ TWO ◊

Is It Our War?

1939-1941

Jack had been traveling in Europe during the spring and summer of 1939. He had obtained permission from Harvard to spend the spring term in Europe as part of his work for his major in political science. After visiting his family and talking to his father in London, Jack went on an unofficial journey of observation for the ambassador. He spent several months in Paris, then traveled to Poland, Latvia, the Soviet Union, Turkey, Palestine, the Balkans, and Belgium. Everywhere he went he talked to people on the street as well as to officials at the various embassies.

Ambassador Kennedy continued to speak out against the United States becoming involved in what he considered European politics — thus losing his popularity with the British, who wanted U.S. support. In his opinion, England and France didn't stand a chance against the well-trained and well-equipped Nazi German army. He continued to advise President Roosevelt against U.S. participation in the war.

On September 3, 1939, Ambassador Kennedy was awakened by a telephone call in the middle of the night. He was told that an unarmed British passenger ship, the *Athenia*, had been torpedoed by a German submarine. Many Americans—310—had been aboard.

The ambassador woke Jack, who had been sleeping in the next room, and told him what had happened. Survivors were being taken to Glasgow, Scotland. He wanted Jack to leave at once for Glasgow to help the survivors and to find out exactly what had occurred. It was a big job for a 22-year-old.

When Jack reached Glasgow he found a scene of tragedy, courage, and indignation. Some of the passengers wanted the U.S. government to send a warship for them. Jack explained that the United States had not declared war on Germany, so sending a battleship would be against international law. He assured them that space would be found for them on other ships. Jack was just as angry as they were at the attack on an unarmed passenger ship.

As the war progressed, the ambassador became concerned about protecting his family. To ensure their safety, he sent his family home to the United States, but he stayed at his post in London.

That fall Jack returned to Harvard a much more mature and thoughtful young man. He began to study with real purpose for the first time in his life. Professor Arthur N. Holcombe, who taught political science, wrote of Jack's scholarship:

> He had a genuine and deep interest in ideas, and courses which presented ideas so as to bring out their practical importance in life. . . . When he had work to

Jack, far right, *holding his hat and suitcase, jokes with some friends on the campus of Harvard University.*

do which interested him, he threw all his great energy and fine intelligence into it, producing results of superior quality.

Jack missed the earlier, carefree times he'd had with his friends, and he missed playing football. As a Harvard freshman, he had been first-string end on the freshman squad. He and his friend Torb McDonald had practiced passing and receiving until they were so good that the coach had used them as the opposing offense in practice games against the varsity team. In one of the practice games against the bigger, stronger varsity team, Jack received an injury to his back that caused him much suffering for the rest of his life.

However, Jack realized that other things were more important than sports just now. It was time to write his senior

Jack's thesis, "Appeasement at Munich," became a best-seller when it was published in 1940 as a book called Why England Slept. *He became a successful author at age 25.*

thesis. Jack had been thinking a great deal about England, Hitler, and the apathy—the lack of concern—on the part of the British people before the war. He began to put his thoughts on paper. After much studying, writing, and rewriting, he finished his thesis, "Appeasement at Munich." The paper was outstanding in its analysis of Europe's and

England's crisis. Two of Jack's professors thought it was good enough to be published.

In June 1940, Jack graduated *cum laude* (with praise or distinction) from Harvard. His thesis earned a *magna cum laude* (great praise). Mr. Kennedy could not leave his post in London, but Rose Kennedy and all Jack's sisters went to Boston for the festivities of commencement week.

After graduation, Jack began to send his paper to publishers, and it was accepted on the second try. Wilfrid Funk published it under the title *Why England Slept*. It became a best-seller. Jack, at 25, became a literary sensation.

The summer of 1940 in Hyannis Port was the last time the Kennedy family (except for the ambassador) would all be together, and they seemed to sense it. The games of touch football and tennis, the swimming and sailing went on at a furious pace. Family discussions at Hyannis Port centered around the part the United States would or should play in World War II. It was the same topic people were talking about all over the land. Should we get into the fight? Was it our war?

Only Rosemary stood outside the charmed circle. It had gradually become apparent to the Kennedys that the oldest daughter was not like the rest of the family. Rosemary was retarded. She had wild, violent moods, and she was retreating into a world of her own. That fall she had a lobotomy, a neurosurgical operation. Although it eliminated her wild moods, it also seemed to increase her retardation. Finally she was confined to a home for the mentally retarded in Wisconsin.

In Europe the Nazi armies had overtaken the Netherlands, Denmark, and Romania. France had fallen. Only the poorly armed British army stood in the way of a German victory over all of Europe. The United States was sending supplies and war materials, but it had not yet formally declared war.

Joseph Kennedy still didn't want the United States to become involved in the war. His popularity decreased in England and also in many circles in the United States because of his opposition to the war. He had lost President Roosevelt's friendship as well. In October 1940, he resigned his post as ambassador and returned to the United States. The family welcomed him back and tried to make him feel better.

Both Jack and Joe wanted to volunteer in the armed services. In the spring, Joe had been accepted as a naval air cadet. Jack was turned down by both the army and the navy because of his back trouble and history of illness. So many times his plans had been set back because of illness and pain! But he used his fighting spirit to overcome those obstacles. He bought special gym equipment and barbells and worked out every day. Each morning he took a cross-country run. He was determined to build up his weak back muscles.

Jack had been around water and small boats most of his life. He felt sure that the navy could use his experience. In September he tried again. This time he made it, but, much to his disgust, he was assigned to a desk job in Washington. That wasn't what Jack wanted at all. He applied for a transfer.

On December 7, 1941, an act occurred that finally brought the United States into World War II. The Japanese air force carried out a surprise attack on the United States naval fleet at Pearl Harbor, Hawaii. Most of the fleet was destroyed, and many seamen were killed.

Six months later Jack was sent to the Naval Officers Training School at Northwestern University in Evanston, Illinois. Later he was assigned to the Motor Torpedo Boat Center at Melville, Rhode Island.

One day on the grounds of the center, Jack noticed a game of touch football. It was a free period for Jack, so he strolled over and asked if he could get in the game. The young man who was calling the plays, Paul Fay, thought Jack was a high school kid. He was dressed in an inside-out Harvard sweater, baggy trousers, and sneakers.

The "kid" turned out to be a fast and furious player— "all knees and elbows," Fay said later. Much to Fay's embarrassment, the tall, thin young man turned out to be Fay's instructor in small boat handling!

Jack (standing far right in top photo), *commander of PT 109, poses with his crew. PT boats* (bottom photo) *were fast and easy to maneuver, but they did not offer much protection to the crew aboard them.*

◊ THREE ◊

This Is What It's Like

1941-1944

The PT (patrol torpedo) boat was a fast, light, 80-foot (24-meter)-long motorboat made of plywood. It had four torpedo tubes and carried four 50-caliber machine guns and an antiaircraft gun. It moved easily in and out of the twisting waterways around the small islands that make up the Solomon Islands in the South Pacific. Because of its light construction, a PT boat gave little protection to its crew. PT crews depended on the boat's speed of 40 knots per hour and its ability to maneuver to escape harm from enemy boats.

On the island of Tulagi in late April 1943, Lieutenant John F. Kennedy was put in command of PT 109, a dirty, weather-beaten veteran of the Guadalcanal battles. (Guadalcanal had been a Japanese stronghold, and the Americans had captured it after a bitter struggle.) Jack was dismayed at his first sight of PT 109. He immediately ordered that the boat be put into dry dock for cleaning and repairs.

One holdover from the former crew was still there: Leonard Thom, former football star at Ohio State. Jack made Ensign Thom his executive officer, and together they chose a crew. The PT boat operation was an informal one. Crews changed often from boat to boat as the vulnerable vessels came into the nearby base at Lumberi for repairs or were damaged beyond repair.

Machinist's Mate First Class William Johnson voiced the general opinion of the crew when he said, "Just another 90-day wonder from the states," about their youthful-looking commander. The men soon changed their minds. In contrast to his brother Joe, who demanded "Aye, aye, sir" and other formalities of rank from his air crew, Jack had a more casual style. The PT crew liked Jack because he treated them fairly and worked harder than any of them. They scraped, sanded, and painted the hull, engine room, and lower quarters of PT 109. With the engine cleaned and oiled, and with a coat of fresh, forest-green paint, PT 109 was ready for duty.

United States forces were working a slow passage through the Solomon Sea toward Rabaul, a Japanese stronghold. Rabaul was not far from New Guinea, the ultimate goal of the Americans. PT 109 was already a veteran of seven night patrols and one enemy bombing. On the night of August 1, 1943, word came that the "Tokyo Express," Japanese ships that made periodic raids through the waters of the Solomons, was coming again. A fleet of 15 PT boats was sent out to intercept the Japanese.

There was something eerie about those night patrols down shadowy streams, overhung with tropical growth. The only sounds were the screams of exotic tropical birds, the occasional splash of a crocodile, and the hushed drone of the engine. The water was fairly luminous, and the crews couldn't be sure if a dark shape was an enemy ship, a trick of light or shadow, or another PT boat.

To reduce noise, PT 109 crept along on one engine. Lieutenant Kennedy peered into the darkness. On the foredeck, Engineer John Maguire said his prayers. Ensign Ross stood over a 37-millimeter gun the crew had lashed to the foredeck. Ross had been a last-minute volunteer to the crew. Nineteen-year-old Harold Marney, newest member of the crew, was in the forward gun turret. Suddenly he shouted, "Ship at two o'clock!"

A Japanese destroyer, the *Amagiri*, was almost on top of them. Kennedy ordered Maguire, "Sound general quarters!" It was too late. There was no time to launch a torpedo or to change course. The *Amagiri's* steel hull caused a grinding crunch as it tore into the plywood frame of PT 109. Marney was crushed to death. Jack was hurled against the wall of the cockpit so hard it almost broke his back. His first thought, he related afterward, was, "This is what it's like to be killed."

The *Amagiri* had cut PT 109 in two in the same way a sharp knife slices an apple. The stern, or back half of the boat, was engulfed in flames. The bow section, the front, was still afloat. Because Jack was afraid that fire would break out in the bow, he ordered everyone into the water. Ross, Mauer, and Maguire were with Kennedy in the bow. Jack swam out to search for survivors. The raging flames against the black sky were almost blinding. Even the water was on fire from spilled gasoline.

It took almost superhuman effort to get the men, exhausted and injured, back onto the still-afloat bow. Pat McMahon had been seriously burned. Jack called roll and found everyone present except Marney and Kirksey. They had been killed in the crash.

Until dawn the 11 survivors huddled in the bow and tried to decide what to do. In the dark they didn't know their exact location, and many of the small islands on both sides of Blackett Strait were inhabited by the Japanese. As the shadows lifted they were in danger of being seen by the enemy.

Then what was left of PT 109 overturned, pitching them all into the water. Fortunately Jack had taken inventory of what supplies they had left. Besides a blinker light, they had a ship's lantern, several life jackets, a Thompson machine gun, some small arms, and three knives. They would have to swim to an island, but McMahon had third-degree burns over half his body and couldn't possibly make it alone. Jack and his crew now faced the worst of their ordeal.

Jack kept one knife and gave the other two to Ross and Thom, the other officers. He cut one end of McMahon's life jacket strap. Jack put the loose end of the strap into his mouth and clamped down hard with his teeth. Slipping under McMahon, Jack began to swim while towing McMahon on his back. He said nothing about his own back injury. The others tied what supplies they had to a plank of wood. They used the wooden plank for support in the water as they swam.

Jack's strong, steady strokes soon took him and McMahon out of sight of the others. As he swam, Jack wondered if his crew was following him. Time began to blur. Jack had no idea he had been in the water for eight hours. Then he caught sight of an island. He could tell from its size and shape that it was Plum Pudding Island. The tall casuarina trees would hide them from Japanese planes.

Trying to ignore the pain in his back, Jack reached the rocky shore. Crawling over the sharp coral rock was almost as hard as the swim. McMahon's feet were so blistered he had to crawl on his hands and knees. The two men fell,

Jack was a naval lieutenant and commander of PT 109.

exhausted, under some bushes and rested while they waited for the others. At last Jack sat up and looked out across the water. He was overjoyed to see the plank, with nine bobbing heads alongside, nearing the shore.

They too fell headlong on the shore and rested or slept. Later they found that the island was full of birds, but they couldn't find any eatable plants or water. Jack realized they couldn't stay there long.

After sundown Jack swam out into Ferguson Passage. He hoped to be able to hail a patrolling PT boat. He hadn't had anything to eat or drink for 18 hours. His back was burning with pain. He wore shoes that he had salvaged from the wreck and carried a revolver tied around his neck.

After treading water for hours, Jack was forced to admit that no patrol boats were coming. When he started to swim back, he was caught in a current and swept around in circles. He spotted another small island. He had just enough strength to swim to it. There he collapsed and slept. After a few hours he woke up and swam back to Plum Pudding Island. Jack told Ross, the next best swimmer, to search again for a PT rescue boat that night. Then Jack fell asleep.

Ross started out earlier, so it would still be light in the passage. He waited there just as Jack had done, with no better luck. Where were the PT boats? Wasn't anyone even looking for them?

The next day the entire crew swam to another island, closer to Ferguson Passage. Jack again towed McMahon. On Olasana they found coconut palm trees. A few of the stronger

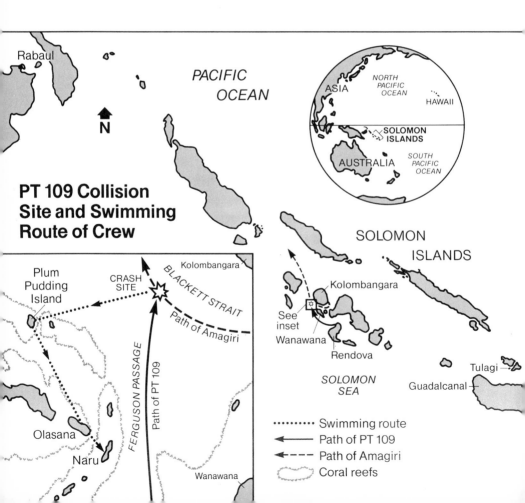

PT 109 Collision Site and Swimming Route of Crew

.... Swimming route
◄——— Path of PT 109
◄– – – Path of Amagiri
〰 Coral reefs

men climbed the trees and shook down some coconuts. They smashed them on the coral rocks and drank the milk eagerly. But after three days of no food or drink, they got sick.

Jack tried hard to keep up the spirits of the men, but they all knew their situation was full of danger. At night it grew cold and they huddled close together to keep warm. During the night Jack heard someone moan, "We're all going to die."

The next day Jack and Ross set off for Naru, an island whose far side overlooked the passage. It was thought to be inhabited by Japanese, but Jack was desperate enough to chance it. When they landed on a sandy shore, they found a cache of rainwater, a large wooden box of hard candy, and a canoe. The cache, or hidden supplies, had been left there by native scouts.

While Jack and Ross were examining their find, two native Melanesian boys approached the island in a small canoe. Each party thought the other was Japanese. The two Melanesians turned their canoe around and headed for Olasana, where Jack had left the rest of his crew.

The canoe that Jack and Ross had found was just big enough for one person, plus the cache. Ross stayed on Naru while Jack started back to Olasana. A tropical storm was brewing, but Jack was sure he could beat it. Although waves picked up the frail canoe and tossed it up and down, Jack knew the fresh supplies would put new heart into the men.

When Jack arrived at Olasana, there was a cheerful fire burning on the shore. The Melanesians had arrived before Jack and had shared some native food with the happy crew. Leonard Thom, the big, blond ex-football star, had waded out into the water and convinced the canoeists that the crew was friendly.

Jack couldn't stay to celebrate with them. He had to hurry back to Naru where he had left Ross. The Melanesians took him back in their canoe. They covered Jack with leaves to hide him in case they were seen by the Japanese. Finally a huge wave picked them up and deposited them on the shore of Naru.

Jack picked up a coconut, scraped off some of the shell, and carved a message. It said:

NARU ISL./
NATIVE KNOWS POSIT [position]
HE CAN PILOT/ 11 ALIVE/
NEED SMALL BOAT
　　　　　　　　　KENNEDY

Jack pointed to Rendova Peak, which could be seen all over the area, and said, "Rendova." The boys seemed to understand.

Unknown to Jack, the boys were scouts, working for Lieutenant Reginald Evans, an Australian coast watcher. (A network of coast watchers hidden in the Solomon Islands watched for enemy ships and planes and reported their positions to Allied ships in the area.) The scouts took the message to Evans. Evans then sent another scout in a canoe with food, water, and a message for Kennedy. Through Evans a plan was set up, and a PT boat was sent to the rescue.

When their rescuers appeared, Jack couldn't help voicing what he and his crew had been thinking.

"Where the devil have you guys been?" Jack shouted.

Someone on the PT boat called back, "Jack, we've got some food for you."

"No thanks," Jack answered. "I've just had a coconut."

The crew of PT 109 was given a hero's welcome when they got to Rendova, but Jack would have none of it.

Jack kept the coconut shell, left, *with his message carved on it on his desk.* Right, *Captain F.L. Conklin presented the Navy and Marine Corps Medal to Jack at the Chelsea Naval Hospital in Massachusetts.*

"We lost two good men," he said. "They are the heroes. The rest of us are alive."

Jack refused home leave and was given another boat, PT 59. Some of his old crew volunteered to serve with him. They continued the strenuous work of patrolling. Twice they took part in rescues of marine patrols.

Jack was in constant pain from his back injury. Eventually he contracted malaria, became very ill, and lost 25 pounds. Even he had to admit that he was no longer fit for duty. He was forced to give up his command and was sent home to Chelsea Naval Hospital near Hyannis Port.

Jack received the Purple Heart, the Navy and Marine Corps Medal, and a citation from Admiral W. F. Halsey.

The citation read, in part:

> For heroism in the rescue of three men following the
> ramming and sinking of his motor torpedo boat . . . on
> the night of August 1-2, 1943. Lieutenant KENNEDY,
> Captain of the boat, directed the rescue of the crew
> and personally rescued three men. . . . His courage,
> endurance and excellent leadership contributed to
> the saving of several lives and was in keeping with the
> highest traditions of the United States Naval Service.

Jack was allowed to leave the hospital on weekends to
spend time with the family at Hyannis Port. It seemed almost
like old times, except that Joe, Kathleen, whom Jack always
called "Kick," and Rosemary weren't there. Young Joe
Kennedy was flying dangerous missions for the Allies along
the coast of Belgium and feeling somewhat jealous of his
younger brother's accomplishments and celebrity. Against
the wishes of her Catholic parents, Kathleen had married an
English officer, a Protestant, whose family was a member of
the British aristocracy.

Jack's back didn't get any better, and he was weak and
tired. Finally he decided to follow his doctors' advice, and he
had an operation on his spine in the summer of 1944. The
operation didn't go well, and Jack was flat on his back in a
hospital bed when he received the worst blow of all. Joseph
P. Kennedy, Jr., had been killed in action!

Joe had been eligible for home leave, but he had volunteered for a special mission. He and a copilot were to take a
plane loaded with explosives over a German submarine base.
A remote control was supposed to have set off the explosives
after the flyers had parachuted from the plane, but something
went wrong. The bombs went off too soon. Joe and his partner
were blown up along with the plane.

Joe, Jr., Jack's older brother, was killed in the war in 1944 while flying a special mission.

Joe's accident happened on August 12, 1944, a little more than a year after the PT 109 collision. The news set back Jack's recovery. Lying there in a hospital bed, Jack thought about Joe, his charm, his cockiness, his gentleness, his kindness. He decided to write a book about Joe. He called it "As We Remember Joe." It was written just for the family and a few close friends. In it he said, "Joe was the star of our family. He did everything better than the rest of us. . . . Through it all he had a deep and abiding faith. . . . He was never far from God."

Jack fought his grief and ill health, but only a month later Kathleen's husband was killed in France. Kathleen was home with the family in Hyannis Port when she got the news. They all drew closer together in their sorrow.

Jack had always thought of his brother Bobby as a freckle-faced kid, but Bobby was growing up. After Joe's death, Bobby resigned from the officers' training program at Harvard and asked for service on the new destroyer USS *Joseph P. Kennedy*, named after his dead brother. His request was granted.

◊ FOUR ◊

Hitting the
Campaign Trail

1944-1956

In November 1944, Franklin Delano Roosevelt was elected president for a fourth term. One of Roosevelt's favorite projects was the establishment of the United Nations, an organization dedicated to world peace and the betterment of humanity. Just two weeks before the United Nations Conference was to meet, President Roosevelt died suddenly. Vice President Truman became president.

The United Nations was to hold its first official meeting in San Francisco, California, in April 1945. The Hearst newspapers, a chain of newspapers owned by William Randolph Hearst, needed a correspondent with foreign experience to report on the meeting. Would Jack do it? Jack was glad to accept.

Jack went to San Francisco with a feeling that perhaps this was something important. He wanted to be where the action was. He watched the proceedings with a keen eye but was soon disappointed. Delegates from the various countries spent more time arguing among themselves than getting down to business. Jack compared it to an international football game, with Secretary of State Edward Stettinius of the United States and England's Anthony Eden trying to tackle Soviet diplomat Vyacheslav Molotov.

"We are beginning to realize how long and difficult the road is ahead," he wrote, meaning that getting many different countries to cooperate was not easy.

Months passed, and although the war in Europe was winding down, Japan still fought on. The Allies sent an order to Japan to surrender, but Japan ignored it. President Truman then decided to use the atomic bomb to hasten the end of the war. United States bombers dropped the first atomic bomb on Hiroshima on August 6, 1945. When Japan still did not surrender, the second atomic attack was launched on Nagasaki on August 9. Terrible damage was done to the cities and the people in them. However, the bombing attacks did bring about the end of the war.

On August 15, people in the United States went wild with joy at the news of Japan's surrender. People danced in the streets and celebrated all night. It was not until September 2 that a formal treaty of surrender was signed in the presence of General Douglas MacArthur, commander-in-chief of forces in the Pacific. The ceremony took place on board the United States battleship *Missouri*.

Now the war was over, and Jack was finished with college and with his military service. But he was still feeling his way in a quickly changing world—a world that would never be the same as it had been before the war. Old attitudes and

The official statement of Japan's surrender was signed by foreign minister Mamoru Shigemitsu aboard the battleship Missouri *on September 2, 1945.*

ideas were giving way to new ones. New, independent nations were emerging in Africa and Asia. The United States and the Soviet Union were engaged in a struggle for power. World events were exciting, and Jack wanted to be a part of them.

Both Jack's grandfathers had been active in politics. Grandfather Fitzgerald, known as Honey Fitz, had been alderman, councilman, mayor of Boston, a state legislator, and a United States congressman. Grandfather Patrick Kennedy had been a state representative and a state senator. At different times he had been fire commissioner, street commissioner, and election commissioner of Boston. The family—particularly Jack's father—had assumed that Joe, Jr., would carry on the family tradition and go into politics. Now, suddenly, Jack was the oldest Kennedy of his generation, and that expectation fell on his shoulders. Jack felt that he had to fill his older brother's shoes, although he also felt that he could never do things quite as well as Joe would have done them.

Jack's chance to get into politics came when Congressman James Curley from the 11th District of Massachusetts decided to retire. The 11th District was a mix of factories, tenements, churches, saloons, shipping wharfs, and Harvard University. Jack declared his intention to run for Congress. He had connections with the old-line politicians through his father and grandfathers, but he also went to the people.

Jack was friendly, but shy and reserved. He thought his parents felt that Joe would have done it better. It wasn't easy for him to walk into a tavern or factory and talk to the workers, but he did it. Sometimes he'd get so involved in what they were doing and saying that he'd have to be pried away. He had a genuine curiosity about their lives and families.

One of the people who opened his door to Jack was Dave Powers. Dave was just home from his war service and living with his widowed sister and her eight children in a walk-up, cold-water apartment in the Charlestown section of Boston. Dave was surprised when a tall, young stranger held out his hand and said, "I'm Jack Kennedy. I'm running for Congress. Will you help me?"

Dave became one of Jack's hardest workers. He introduced Jack to people in the neighborhood and took him to meetings. Although Jack wasn't a great speaker, especially in front of large groups, people were impressed by his simplicity and sincerity. With men like Dave Powers, Larry O'Brien, Les Billings (who was a Republican), and his brother Bobby, Jack set up groups of young Democrats throughout the district.

On election day, Jack and his proud Grandmother and Grandfather Fitzgerald walked to the polling place together. Jack won his congressional seat in 1946 by a margin of more than two to one. It put him on the front page of the *New York Times* and in *Time* magazine. He was 29 years old, but looked younger than his age. In Congress he was sometimes mistaken for a Senate page or an elevator operator.

Jack served the people of his district faithfully. His office door was always open. Ted Reardon and a secretary named Mary Davis handled routine business in Congressman Kennedy's office, but often a telephone caller was surprised when the congressman himself answered. Never a careful dresser, he often showed up for work wearing wrinkled trousers and mismatched socks. In contrast, another new congressman, Richard Nixon of California, was a very dapper dresser. They both served on the Education and Labor Committee.

In Congress Jack's voting sometimes reflected his father's opinions. As a new congressman, Jack didn't always know all he should have known about some issues. On other issues, he was unsure of his opinion. But he did have very strong opinions about social and economic issues, such as working conditions, wages, prices, Social Security, housing, aid to veterans and to the aged, and about foreign policy. These issues represented the needs and concerns of his constituency and the promises he had made during his election campaign. On these issues Jack represented the new generation and voted independently of his father's opinions and freely offered advice. Sometimes he even opposed President Truman, a fellow Democrat. Jack fought particularly hard for a bill to help make decent housing available to veterans. When veterans returned from the war, there was an acute shortage

Jack casts his vote with his grandparents, John and Mary Fitzgerald, top. Below, *Honey Fitz, Joe, Sr., and Jack share a moment together.*

of housing. But when housing legislation came up for a vote in Congress, Republicans and Southern Democrats sided with the real estate and construction lobbies and repeatedly defeated bills for low-rent housing projects. Jack often felt angry and frustrated.

Jack sometimes left his office early, put on a sweatshirt and sneakers, and played football or softball with a bunch of boys at a Georgetown playground. One of the players told their coach, "That new kid isn't bad, but he needs a lot of work." Because he looked so young, it was hard for some older congressmen to take him seriously. Although the Kennedy name meant a lot in Boston, it wasn't very important—or even well known—in Washington.

After three two-year terms as a congressman, Jack became frustrated with House rules and customs. It was hard to dramatize his position on an issue, and legislation was often watered down to satisfy many different and opposing factions. He decided to run for the Senate in 1952. His opponent was Republican Senator Henry Cabot Lodge from Massachusetts. Lodge had already served two terms in the Senate. He was 15 years older than Jack Kennedy and was a member of an old, distinguished family in Massachusetts. Honey Fitz had run unsuccessfully for the same Senate seat against Lodge's grandfather in 1916.

At the beginning of the 1952 campaign, Jack's back hurt so much that he was forced to use crutches. The hole left in his back from the last operation had never healed. He looked thin and sickly. It seemed that this handicap might end his career at its very beginning.

Jack's determination, however, was more intense than his pain. He had the will to win. This time he made 27-year-old

Bobby, who had just finished law school, his campaign manager. Except for Honey Fitz, who had died in 1950, the team that had worked so well before was together again.

The Kennedy campaign in Fall River, Massachusetts, was typical of Jack's style. The main industries in Fall River were textile making and ladies' garments. A good many of the residents were of French descent. Ninety percent of them were Republican. Jack made Ed Berube, a bus driver of French descent, his Fall River manager.

At the first Fall River political meeting, the 50th-anniversary party at a local church, Ed Berube stood up to announce the speaker. He said, "Ladies and gentlemen, I'd like you to meet Congressman Joe Martin."

Martin was a Republican. The audience burst into laughter. Poor Ed Berube thought he was finished. Jack joined in the laughter and said, "Maybe Ed would rather be working with Joe Martin, but I'd rather have him working for me." Then Jack spoke to them in French and won their hearts.

Jack was on a hectic schedule. He visited mills and factories, barber shops and small restaurants. He spoke to everyone he could. On one of his Fall River tours, he stopped at a small bakery run by "Babe" Piourde to buy some cupcakes. After tasting them, Jack said, "Babe, if I ever get married, you're going to bake the wedding cake."

Jack's sisters, Eunice, Patricia, and Jean, and often his mother, held teas at which Jack spoke. At one tea a large group of women gathered on a hot July night. After his speech Jack moved around the room to speak to each one of of the women individually, although he was on crutches at the time.

When all the votes were in and tallied on election day in November 1952, Kennedy beat Lodge. Yet in a wave of

Jack, top left, *won the Massachusetts Senate seat of Henry Cabot Lodge,* top right. *He plunged into his Senate job enthusiastically,* bottom.

After the Senate election, Jack saw Jacqueline Bouvier frequently.

increased support for Republicans, Dwight D. Eisenhower won the presidency on the same day and carried Massachusetts by over 200,000 votes. Eisenhower chose Lodge to be United States ambassador to the United Nations.

Shortly before his Senate campaign began, Jack was introduced to a beautiful young lady, Jacqueline Bouvier. She had grown up in New York and Washington and had attended Vassar College and the Sorbonne in Paris, France. Her mother and stepfather lived in Newport, Rhode Island. Jackie's family was Catholic and came from a wealthy background as did Jack's. She spoke French, Italian, and Spanish fluently. Jack was very much attracted to the soft-

The Kennedys cut their wedding cake, while Bobby (to the left of the bride) *and Ted* (extreme left) *offer encouragement.*

spoken, dark-haired Jacqueline, but he didn't see her again for six months. She went to Europe, and Jack was busy campaigning in Massachusetts.

After the election, Jack called her. Jacqueline had just returned to Washington and was working as an inquiring photographer for the *Times-Herald*. They began to see each other frequently. Finally Jack asked her to marry him.

On September 12, 1953, they were married at St. Mary's Catholic Church in Newport, Rhode Island. Jacqueline's mother and stepfather were socially prominent and had a beautiful Newport estate, called Hammersmith Farm, where

Senator Joe McCarthy, left, *accused many people, including some members of the military, of having communist connections.*

the wedding reception was held. The ceremony in the church was performed by Archbishop Richard Cushing of Boston, Rose Kennedy's good friend. Bobby Kennedy was the best man. True to his promise, Jack asked Babe Piourde to make the wedding cake.

Jack plunged into his Senate job with enthusiasm. He and Jacqueline moved into a red brick house at 3307 N Street, one of many similar homes in the Georgetown area of Washington. The front door opened onto a brick sidewalk. The back opened to a walled garden.

During the 1950s, the fear of communism and communist spy plots haunted the country. Anticommunism was a popular political issue. Politicians, including Jack Kennedy, were praised for taking a tough stance on the issue. While in the House of Representatives, Jack had gotten labor representatives to testify about communist influence within their unions. Senator Joe McCarthy of Wisconsin conducted congressional hearings to find out about communist influence in the government, labor unions, and other organizations, but he turned the hearings into "witch hunts." McCarthy accused many innocent people of having communist connections and ruined many lives and careers. As time went on, his charges became wilder and more unfounded. Eventually, a movement to officially censure (or rebuke) him got under way in the Senate. This put Jack in a difficult spot, since his father supported McCarthy and Jack had worked with him in the early stages of the anticommunist movement. Kennedy and Joe McCarthy had been freshman congressmen together.

On December 2, 1954, when the Senate voted on the matter, Jack was too sick to be there. His back had become extremely painful once more. He had also been diagnosed as having Addison's disease, a glandular deficiency that lowers the body's resistance to infection. A delicate spinal operation would be a life-threatening procedure. Several doctors refused to operate. Dr. Philip Wilson finally consented but gave Jack only a 50-50 chance of survival.

On October 21, 1954, the operation took place at the Hospital for Special Surgery in New York. An infection set in, and Jack lapsed into a coma and was at the point of death. Jacqueline and all the members of the family stood at his bedside while the last rites of the Catholic church were given to him.

Surprisingly, Jack rallied and was well enough by December to be flown to the family's Palm Beach home for Christmas. His back would not heal, however, and in February 1955 he was flown back to the hospital for another operation. This time it was successful.

While he was still flat on his back and recovering from the surgery, Jack began to write *Profiles in Courage*, a book showing examples of moral courage in the lives of eight senators who risked their careers for a great cause or a belief. Jacqueline visited him every day, brought him reference books, took dictation, and read his work back to him. Ted Sorensen, Kennedy's speech writer and legislative aide, also helped, and several authorities added their expertise.

When *Profiles in Courage* was published in 1956 it bore a dedication, "To my wife, Jacqueline, whose help during all the days of my convalescence I cannot ever adequately acknowledge." Jack also paid tribute to Ted Sorensen for his help. *Profiles in Courage* made the best-seller list and was even more successful than *Why England Slept*. It won the Pulitzer Prize (an annual prize given for excellence in several categories of American literature) for biography.

The day that Jack was able to return to his Senate office was a happy one for him. He rode the little, chrome-railed subway car from his office to the Senate chamber, although a dutiful guard told him, "It's just for senators." When he walked into the Senate, with its four semicircular rows of desks, the entire Senate rose to its feet and applauded to welcome him back. Senator Lyndon Johnson, Democratic leader of the Senate, gave a welcoming speech. Senator William Knowland, Republican leader, added his good wishes. With a broad smile on his face, Jack took his seat in a back row.

One day, in the Senate caucus room, Senator Kennedy noticed a group of high school students in the hall. When he learned they were from Massachusetts, he invited them into the hearing room to observe congressional procedure first-hand. He served his constituents in any way he could.

Jack was beginning to make his mark in the Senate. He was well informed and able to see both sides of an issue. He always weighed his decisions carefully. For this he was sometimes called a "cold fish," meaning he didn't feel strongly about anything. But that was far from the truth.

Jack believed strongly in the right of every person to get a good education, to have an equal opportunity for jobs, and to have a decent standard of living. On May 17, 1954, the Supreme Court had handed down its famous decision on school desegregation. The Court ruled that segregation in public schools was unconstitutional. There could no longer be separate schools for black children. Enforcement of the decision moved very slowly, hardly at all in the Southern states. Southern Democratic senators and conservative Republicans voted down any meaningful, new civil rights legislation. Someone was going to have to take a stand and lead the country into an era of greater civil rights.

Jack made the nomi-
nating speech for Adlai
Stevenson at the 1956
Democratic National
Convention, below.
Jacqueline sometimes
helped Jack campaign,
right.

◊ FIVE ◊

On His Way

1956-1960

In his second term in the Senate, Jack quickly assumed a position of leadership. He became a member of the powerful Senate Foreign Relations Committee. In a speech on the Senate floor, he said, "International events today are subject to a double pull—a search for political identity by the new states and a search for unity among the established states of the world. As Europe draws in upon itself toward a common market and greater political integration, Africa, its former colonial state, is breaking apart into new and emergent states."

Jack was also chairman of the Senate Subcommittee on Labor. Jack guided his Labor Reform Bill to a 90-1 victory in Senate debate. He was known as a young man in a hurry. His office, Room 362 in the Senate Office Building, seemed to be one of the busiest spots in Washington. It was crowded with

Adlai Stevenson was the Democratic candidate for president in 1956.

people, books, papers, posters on the wall, and souvenirs of PT 109. Somehow, among all the hustle and bustle, the work got done.

When the Democratic National Convention was held in Chicago in 1956, there was some talk of Jack Kennedy as a possible candidate for vice president. He was asked to make the nominating speech for Adlai Stevenson, who was again running as the Democratic presidential candidate against Eisenhower. It was Jack Kennedy's first nationwide television appearance. He did so well that everyone seemed sold on him—everyone except Stevenson and Senator Estes Kefauver of Tennessee, who wanted to be vice president himself.

Kefauver won the nomination for vice president by a small margin. It was Jack's first defeat. Jack's father had warned him not to try for the vice presidential nomination. "Leave it alone, Jack," he had said. "Stevenson's a loser."

Events proved he was right. The Stevenson-Kefauver ticket suffered a crushing defeat in the November election.

Jack had reason to be glad he had lost the nomination. He went back to his job in the Senate with renewed determination to do the best he could possibly do, as his father had always taught him.

Late in 1957, the Kennedy hopes for a child were answered when Caroline was born. The quiet, three-story home on N Street in Georgetown now had a nursery, a baby carriage, and a proud father. Jack delighted in each stage of Caroline's development. With the birth of Caroline, Jacqueline seemed happier than ever before in her married life. She was a radiant young mother.

Jack and his brother Bobby found themselves more and more in the news in the late '50s. Bobby was chief counsel for the Senate Investigations Subcommittee, chaired by Senator John McClellan. When this committee uncovered corrupt labor practices, a new subcommittee, sometimes

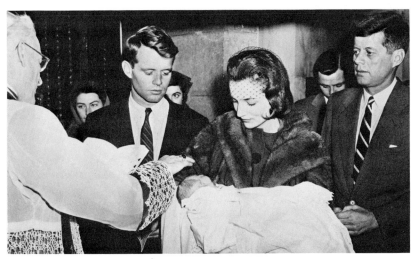

Caroline Kennedy was christened on December 13, 1957 by Cardinal Cushing. Lee Radziwill, Jacqueline's sister, is holding the baby. Bobby is to the left, Jack to the right.

Both Jack (center) *and Bobby* (left) *served on a Senate subcommittee to investigate corrupt labor practices.*

called the Rackets Committee, was formed to look into the matter more closely. McClellan and Bobby carried over their roles to the new subcommittee. Because Jack was on the Senate Labor Committee, he was chosen as one of four senators on the new subcommittee. Both brothers worked closely together and became known to the public during the televised hearings.

An eighth-grade girl in Chicago, Kathleen Ann Corley, watched the hearings and decided to write to the two handsome Kennedys. She addressed her letter to John and Robert Kennedy.

Kathie was the envy of all her classmates when she received two letters and two autographed photographs. In the midst of the Senate hearings, both brothers took time to answer the letter of a young stranger. Jack's letter follows:

John F. Kennedy   United States Senate   Committees:
                                             Foreign Relations
                                             Labor
                                             Public Welfare

July 22, 1958

Miss Kathleen Corley
8811 S. Beverly
Chicago 20, Ill.

Dear Kathleen,

This will acknowledge and thank you for your most kind letter of recent date. I very much appreciate the interest and thoughtfulness which prompted you to write, and, at your request, I am enclosing an autographed photograph.

Inasmuch as your letter was also addressed to my brother, Bob, I am forwarding it directly to him.

With every good wish, I am

Sincerely yours,

John F. Kennedy

Jack was emerging as a person in his own right. It had taken a long time to rid himself of the belief that he was only a poor substitute for his brother Joe. Now he was no longer in Joe's shadow. In fact, he had many qualities that Joe had lacked. He was known for his sharp wit, his remarkable command of facts, and—best of all—his ability to laugh at himself. He cared passionately about poor people, old people, and victims of unfairness all over the country and the world. He had tried to do something to help through legislation. Then he decided to try for a more powerful job: that of the president. He thought that, as president, he would have a much better chance of reaching his goals.

He started taking novocaine injections to reduce his back pain and a new medication to help control his Addison's disease. His health had improved a good deal. He felt strong and full of energy. Although he would always have a painful back, no one would think to look at the smiling, handsome, confident young man that he was in pain.

Jack began speaking to groups all over the country. In six weeks during the fall of 1956, he made more than 150 speeches and appearances and traveled in 24 states. At first he campaigned for Adlai Stevenson, but after Stevenson's defeat in November, he continued his speeches on his own behalf. He wanted to become better known outside of Massachusetts. In fact, he wanted to visit every state in the country. It was no secret that Jack had his eye on the presidency.

Jacqueline didn't like the frantic pace of campaigning or the way a campaign disrupted family life. She knew that Jack would have to be away from home even more than his usual Senate business required. Jacqueline disliked being alone so much of the time, but she didn't want to discourage her husband, so she tried to do her part.

Between 1956 and 1960, Jack talked to coal miners in West Virginia, dairy farmers in Wisconsin, labor leaders in Chicago, politicians in New York. Everywhere he went, he found his Catholic religion raised doubt and suspicion in voters. People were afraid that the pope, who resides in Rome, Italy, and is the head of the Catholic church, would run the country. No Catholic had ever been president. Only one Catholic had ever run for that office—Al Smith of New York—and he had been soundly beaten in 1928.

At a meeting held at a high school in a far western state, the matter came out into the open. A student stood up and asked, "Senator Kennedy, can a Catholic become president?"

Jack replied that he had taken an oath of loyalty to his

country when he entered the navy, when he became a congressman, and when he became a senator. "If I was qualified to serve my country in those other capacities, I am qualified to serve it as president." He added, "No one asked my brother Joe if he had divided loyalties when he volunteered and died for his country." The audience applauded his answer.

By 1959 the campaign was running in high gear. Jack bought a plane (called the *Caroline* after his daughter) so he would always have rapid transportation. His campaign staff was working smoothly. His manager was Bobby. Ted Sorensen, Larry O'Brien, Ken O'Donnell, Dave Powers, Steve Smith (later his sister Jean's husband), and Pierre Salinger, recently added as press secretary, also played important roles.

The presidential primary elections began early in March in New Hampshire, where Kennedy won with a record vote—more than twice the previous record. Primary elections test the voters' preference for a presidential candidate. Two or more candidates of the same political party compete for votes. In many states, winning a primary election means a candidate wins the pledges of delegates to the national convention, where the party's presidential nominee is selected. Kennedy knew he needed those delegate votes.

Senator Hubert Humphrey of Minnesota, who also wanted to be president, entered the Wisconsin primary. Jack decided to challenge him there. Bobby advised Jack not to do it. Humphrey was very well known in Wisconsin. Not only are Wisconsin and Minnesota neighboring states, they also share many similarities. For example, both are dairy and farming states. Jack was in no sense a farm boy. The religious question was also a big obstacle since many residents of both states are of Protestant German and Scandinavian descent.

Jack went ahead with his plan. In bitter, wintry cold he walked the streets of small towns in Wisconsin. At first people seemed to disappear as he approached. Everyone knew that Kennedy was a rich man's son. He flew in on his own plane. Humphrey came on a bus.

Gradually the picture changed. Crowds kept getting larger. People began to realize that this "rich man's son" cared about them. He was informed about the problems of the farmer, the small dairy operator, and people in small businesses. People said that he had a "good head on his shoulders." He cared about the unemployed and about decent wages and living conditions. On primary day, April 5, 1960, Wisconsin Democrats chose Kennedy as their presidential candidate over Humphrey by 106,000 votes.

Kennedy and Humphrey were opponents again in the West Virginia primary. The state faced pressing problems of poverty, unemployment, and health care, which had to be discussed. Also, in a state where only 3 percent of the population were Catholic, the religious issue was very important to the voters. Kennedy had to answer questions about his religion again and again.

Jack explained that he believed in the right of each person to worship as he or she pleased and in the separation of church and state, which limits the powers and concerns of government to secular affairs and forbids the government to establish, promote, or prohibit any specific religion. On May 10, when West Virginians went to the polls, they gave Kennedy 212,000 votes to 136,000 for Humphrey. Humphrey withdrew as a presidential candidate.

Jack continued a strenuous schedule of speaking engagements, from one end of the country to the other. The 50-member Council of Methodist Bishops met in Washington

Jack and Hubert H. Humphrey both wanted to be the Democratic nominee for president. Below, *Jack campaigns for the West Virginia primary.*

in April 1959 and invited Jack to attend. There he was quizzed on his religion and its possible effect on his ability to hold office.

"I am a strong Catholic," Jack replied.

> I come from a strong Catholic family. But I regret the fact that some people get the idea that the Catholic church favors a church-state tie.
>
> I will make my decisions according to my own judgment of the best interests of all the people. I do not intend to disavow either my religion or my beliefs in order to win the presidency. If the outcome of this campaign was settled on the day I was born, then the whole nation is the loser.

The bishops applauded his talk. They admitted that they admired his honesty, courage, and his impartial attitude. It was quite a victory for Jack.

Senator Humphrey was out of the running, but a number of other prominent Democrats were giving Jack strong competition. Among them were Senator Stuart Symington of Missouri, Senator Lyndon Johnson of Texas, and Governor Pat Brown of California.

Several weeks before the Democratic convention, the Republican party held its convention. Republican delegates had nominated Richard Nixon, Eisenhower's vice president, as their presidential candidate. Nixon and Jack had been freshman congressmen together.

The Democratic National Convention in Los Angeles, California, in 1960 was noisy and colorful. Aides of Senator Lyndon Johnson gave out orchids. Senator Symington's workers handed out adhesive bandages printed with the slogan "Stick with Symington." Fans of Governor Brown served orange juice from California. Not to be outdone, John

Kennedy's workers gave away tie clasps shaped like PT 109.

Behind all the carnival atmosphere, serious men and women were weighing the merits and chances of their candidates. The candidates spoke to delegates from the various states to explain their views. Jack refused to change any of his positions to please a particular group. He was his own man. Not even his father could sway Jack's views.

Balloting, or voting for the candidates, began in the Los Angeles Sports Arena. There were the usual flowery speeches in favor of favorite sons, those who were popular in their own states but were not nationally important. The states were called on to vote, one by one, in alphabetical order.

The magic number was 761—the number of votes a nominee needed to win the presidential nomination. Bobby Kennedy and Jack's aide Larry O'Brien estimated that Jack had a sure 762 votes. But nothing is sure during a presidential convention. Delegates could always change their votes.

In all the noise and banner waving, the straw hats and printed slogans, the voice of the person calling the roll boomed out over the public address system: "Wyoming!"

Jack needed only 11 votes to win. Ten of Wyoming's fifteen votes were pledged to Jack. Younger brother Ted had been campaigning in the western states. Teddy quickly worked his way through the crowd to the Wyoming delegation.

"Ten votes won't do it," Teddy shouted, "but eleven will!"

"Let 'em all go!" the Wyoming chairman yelled. Jack was over the top!

The final vote for Jack was 806, and the convention voted to make it unanimous. Most of the family were there, except Jacqueline, who was expecting another baby, and Jack's father, who had tried to stay in the background during the campaign. Jack's sister Patricia tossed her hat in the air.

Jack chose Lyndon Baines Johnson of Texas to be the vice presidential candidate, although many people advised against it.

Teddy grabbed the Wyoming standard and waved it wildly. Rose Kennedy smiled proudly.

Jack had watched the proceedings on television in a rented apartment. It was customary for candidates not to appear on the floor of the convention until results were final. Jack's car had to inch its way through cheering crowds, reporters, and photographers. A huge traffic jam developed, and it wasn't until the early morning of July 12 that Jack was able to join the rest of the family at the Sports Arena.

People were crying with joy as Jack made his brief acceptance speech. He said, "This is in many ways the most important election in the history of our country. All of us are united in our devotion to this country. We wish to keep it strong and free. It requires the best in all of us. I can assure all of you here who have reposed this confidence in me that I'll be worthy of your trust."

The convention wasn't over yet. A vice presidential candidate had to be chosen. Lyndon Johnson had been Jack's closest rival, with 409 votes. Jack felt sure that Johnson would be the strongest running mate. As a senator from Texas, Lyndon Johnson commanded a large number of votes in the general election, because in 1960 Texas was the largest state in the Union. Jack also hoped that the selection of Johnson might influence some southern and western states. But Bobby and many others were against choosing Johnson as the vice presidential candidate.

The next day all the convention delegates and party leaders were on hand to unite behind their new leader, John Fitzgerald Kennedy. Jack chose Lyndon Johnson to be his vice president. The delegates ratified, or confirmed, his choice.

In his acceptance speech, Johnson said, "I will go wherever John Kennedy wants me to go, because we both want America to follow the same road."

When Kennedy addressed the convention, he introduced the idea of "The New Frontier."

> The New Frontier is here, whether we seek it or not. . . . I believe that the times require imagination and courage and perseverance. I'm asking each of you to be pioneers toward the New Frontier. My call is to the young in heart, regardless of age — to the stout in spirit, regardless of party, to all who respond to the scriptural call, "Be strong and of courage, be not afraid, neither be dismayed."

In his inaugural speech and during his term as president, Jack encouraged young people to become involved in their government.

◊ SIX ◊

"Ask What You Can Do..."

1960-1961

Jack was able to endure 18-hour days. He made brief personal appearances in many small communities and wrote speeches while traveling on his plane, the *Caroline*. In 10 weeks, Jack traveled 78,654 miles (126,554 km). Everywhere he went the crowds got bigger. Young people came to hear him. So did the elderly, the foreign born, and the blacks. To many, John Kennedy was a hero.

Toward the end of the campaign, a series of four debates between Kennedy and Nixon took place. These were the first televised political debates ever to be held. They gave the American public a chance to see and compare both candidates. At the first debate, held in a Chicago television studio, Nixon did not do well. He looked stiff and ill at ease. Nixon presented his ideas well enough, but he did not answer Jack's arguments in a convincing way.

The Kennedy-Nixon political debates were the first to be televised to the nation.

Jack had the advantage of spontaneity, of being able to ad-lib with ease. All the practice he had had in answering questions from high school and college audiences, crowds of coal miners, farmers, and Protestant ministers had sharpened his naturally quick mind. He had facts and figures to back up his arguments. He was no longer the shy young man who hesitantly addressed small groups of Massachusetts voters. He had poise, ease, and wit, and his good looks certainly didn't hurt his prospects. His sincerity impressed TV audiences. Nixon did better in the next three debates, but it was generally agreed that Kennedy was the winner. The debates marked a turning point in the campaign.

His last appearance of the campaign was at a huge rally in the Boston Gardens on the eve of the election. Boston Gardens was the home of the Boston Celtics, a famed basketball team. Jack was an ardent fan. Bob Cousey, one of the stars of the team, had campaigned for Jack in Boston.

In his speech there, Jack said, "…I ask you to join us in all the tomorrows yet to come, in building America, moving America, picking this country of ours up and sending it into the 60s."

The next morning, November 8, 1960, Jack and Jacqueline were at the polls early to cast their votes in Boston, still their legal residence. Then they took a plane to Hyannis Port, where press and television headquarters had been set up at Bobby's house. Most of the Kennedy children had homes of their own on or near the large acreage, known as the Kennedy Compound, in Hyannis Port.

Results were slow coming in. For the first time, computers were being used on a large scale to count votes. At 7:15 A.M. news commentators predicted a lopsided victory for Richard Nixon. An hour later they predicted a Kennedy sweep. Jack and his loyal workers refused to take these early predictions seriously. The eastern states were the first to be heard from. Around midnight Jack had a lead of 2.3 million. Slowly, that lead went down. As returns from the West and Midwest came in, the picture became more confused. Jacqueline, expecting the baby soon, stayed in her own Hyannis Port home. The other Kennedys stood around at Bobby's house, tense and silent.

Jack finally began to gain in electoral votes.(The candidate who gets the most votes within a state wins all of that state's electoral votes—the number of votes a state has based on its population.) At 3:00 A.M., word came that Nixon would make an appearance at the Ambassador Hotel in Los Angeles. The group at Bobby's house all thought that Nixon would concede the election to Kennedy. Instead Nixon said, "If the present trend continues, Mr.—Senator Kennedy will be the next president of the United States."

At 4:00 A.M. everyone went to bed. In the morning there was still no definite word. The only one who was sure of the outcome was young Caroline. When she first saw her father that morning she said, "Good morning, Mr. President." Jack laughed and lifted his daughter high in the air. Then he gave her a piggyback ride down to the beach.

It was a cold, windy November day, but almost all of the Kennedys were out that morning walking along the bleak shore of the Atlantic Ocean. Secret Service men appeared about 7:30 A.M., and Jack took that as a good sign. Secret Service men were always assigned to guard the president.

The family and close friends went back to Bobby's house and grouped around the television. Around noon Minnesota came through for Kennedy. The long wait was over. Jack had won!

All of their lives would be changed. So would the United States—and perhaps the world.

Nixon sent a telegram of congratulations, saying in part, "I know you will have the support of all Americans as you lead the nation in the cause of peace and freedom in the next four years."

Jack could now acknowledge his victory and thank all those who had worked so hard for him and all those who had voted for him. He and Jacqueline and all the Kennedys, campaign workers, friends, and supporters went to the Hyannis Port National Guard Armory, where they were awaited by the press and fans. Jack made a brief speech, read the telegrams of congratulation from Nixon and President Eisenhower, and finished with, "So now my wife and I prepare for a new administration—and for a new baby."

The president-elect and his wife returned to Georgetown, she to await the baby, he to begin forming his staff and cabinet. He put his sister Eunice's husband, Sargent Shriver, aide Larry O'Brien, and Bobby to work seeking out the best possible choices for important posts in the new administration. He also consulted some of his Harvard professors. "I want the best men we can find," he said.

Presidential inaugurations are always held in January. In the weeks between the election and the inauguration, an event took place that took precedence over everything else for the Kennedys. Jacqueline gave birth to a baby boy. They called him John Fitzgerald Kennedy, Jr.

The baby had been born almost a month too soon and had to be in an incubator for nine days. Jack visited the hospital several times a day to see his wife and baby son. When John, Jr., was well and strong enough to travel, Jack, Jacqueline, Caroline, and "Caroline's baby brother" went to Palm Beach, Florida, for the Christmas holidays.

When Jack and his family returned to Georgetown, shortly before the inauguration, the front door of their red brick house was besieged by reporters at all hours. To spare Jacqueline and the rest of the household, Jack got into the habit of meeting reporters at the front door with each announcement of a new appointee. He would stand, hatless and coatless, in the wintry weather, and with his usual good humor answer their questions.

Jack kept J. Edgar Hoover as head of the Federal Bureau of Investigation (FBI) and Allen Dulles as chief of the Central Intelligence Agency (CIA). Jack ignored political boundaries when appointing people to fill important positions. He chose people based on their intelligence and integrity rather than on their party loyalty. He asked Robert McNamara, a Republican, to be secretary of defense, and Douglas Dillon, another Republican, to be secretary of the treasury.

The only appointment Jack hesitated to announce to reporters was that of his brother Bobby. Jack wanted no one but Bobby as attorney general of the United States. Bobby was not easy to persuade. "Come over and have breakfast with me," Jack told him. "Come and see the new baby."

"You know what they'll say," Bobby protested, after he had admired John, Jr., in his crib. "Nepotism, family—all that."

Jack joked, "I'll make the announcement about 2:00 A.M. when no one's around, and then I'll stick my head out and whisper, 'It's Bobby.'"

Both brothers met the press and Jack made the announcement. Immediately they were deluged with just the kind of questions and remarks they had feared. Bobby looked a little flustered, but Jack stayed cool. He explained that he trusted Bobby more than anyone else he could think of—trusted his judgment, his ability, and his commitment. "Besides," he added calmly, but with characteristic wit, "I see no reason why Bobby shouldn't get a little experience before he goes out to practice law."

When the two Kennedys went back into the house, the reporters all trooped across the street to the house of a kind woman who often served them coffee and doughnuts while they warmed up.

The night before Inauguration Day it snowed heavily. In spite of a large crew of workmen who labored all through the night to clear away the snow, many people couldn't get through the snow-clogged streets.

Cars were stranded in snow drifts. Many people walked in snow over their ankles. Somehow everyone made it to their destinations. It all added to the spirit of adventure and excitement that everyone felt.

Jack and Jacqueline stand in the center as members of the Kennedy cabinet are sworn in by Chief Justice Earl Warren.

On the morning of Inauguration Day, Jack went across the street to the kind woman's house. The walks had not yet been shovelled. Great was the woman's surprise when she opened the door and found the bareheaded president-elect with a bronze plaque under his arm.

He had had it made for her to commemorate her kindness to the cold, hungry reporters. He also sent a special car to take her to the inauguration where he had reserved a seat for her. He then continued on to his parish church, Holy Trinity, for Mass.

With cheering crowds lining the still-snowy streets, Jack and Jacqueline left Georgetown to have coffee with the Eisenhowers. Although the president-elect had requested all the men to wear formal attire, he carried his top hat and only once in a while remembered to put it on. The old and new

Chief Justice Earl Warren administers the oath of office to John F. Kennedy, 35th president of the United States. Jacqueline Kennedy is at the far left.

presidential parties arrived at the Capitol steps around 12:30 P.M. A raised platform and reviewing stand had been set up in front of the broad, high Capitol steps.

With his right hand on the family Bible, which had belonged to Grandfather Fitzgerald and to his father before him, John Kennedy swore to uphold the Constitution and the laws of the United States to the best of his ability.

Before he gave his inaugural address, Jack looked out over the vast assemblage of foreign dignitaries, family, friends, ordinary people, and government officials, and introduced the frail, white-haired old man who stood nearby: poet Robert Frost. "I have asked Mr. Frost to come here today to read us his poem because I think he has something important to say."

The poet took a few steps forward to face the microphone. The wind ruffled his wispy, white hair. The wintry sun glanced off the white paper he held in his hand and blinded him. The paper shook as his hand trembled. The young president who had invited him smiled encouragingly. Robert Frost, in a voice suddenly strong, lay down the troublesome paper and recited from memory another poem, "The Gift Outright"— "The land was ours before we were the land's. . . ."

When Frost finished his poem, Jack stepped to the podium to deliver his inaugural address. His face solemn, his voice ringing with conviction, the new president began:

> My fellow Americans: We observe today not a victory of party but a celebration of freedom, symbolizing an end as well as a beginning, signifying renewal as well as change. . . .
>
> We dare not forget today that we are the heirs of that first revolution. Let the word go forth from this time and place, to friend and foe alike, that the torch has been passed to a new generation of Americans, born in this century, tempered by war, disciplined by a hard and bitter peace, proud of our ancient heritage, and unwilling to witness or permit the slow undoing of those human rights to which this nation has always been committed, and to which we are committed today at home and around the world. . . .
>
> In your hands, my fellow citizens, more than mine, will rest the final success or failure of our course. Since this country was founded, each generation of Americans has been summoned to give testimony to its national loyalty. The graves of young Americans who answered the call to service surround the globe.
>
> Now the trumpet summons us again—not as a call to bear arms, though arms we need; not as a call to battle, though embattled we are; but as a call to bear the burden of a long twilight struggle, year in and year out, "rejoicing in hope, patient in tribulation,"

a struggle against the common enemies of man:
tyranny, poverty, disease and war itself. . . .

And so, my fellow Americans: ask not what your
country can do for you; ask what you can do for your
country. . . .

Finally, whether you are citizens of America or
citizens of the world, ask of us here the same high
standards of strength and sacrifice which we ask of
you. With a good conscience our only sure reward, with
history the final judge of our deeds, let us go forth
to lead the land we love, asking His blessing and His
help, but knowing that here on earth God's work must
truly be our own.

To all the audience before him, and to millions of people
watching on television, this new, young president embodied
a fresh spirit, new ideas, dedication, and hope for great things
to come.

A mammoth parade, representing all of the armed services,
various branches of government, events in Jack Kennedy's
life, and many organizations filled the rest of the afternoon.
Jack was thrilled by a PT 109 float with Leonard Thom,
Barney Ross, and other wartime buddies grinning and waving.

As the afternoon wore on, it must have seemed to many
people as though the parade would never end, but Jack seemed
to enjoy every minute of it. He stayed until the last float
passed by, the last band played, the last flag waved.

That evening at the inaugural ball, Jacqueline looked
beautiful in her white gown. She left the festivities around
midnight, but Jack stayed much later, moving from one event
to another and plainly having a good time.

Inaugural festivities included a parade (above) *with a PT 109 float.* Below, *the Kennedys arrive at the inaugural ball.*

The Peace Corps offered volunteers, mainly young people, an opportunity to promote peace and friendship in many parts of the world, as here in Togo, a country in Africa.

◊ SEVEN ◊

The New Frontier

1961-1963

When the excitement and thrill of Inauguration Day ended, Jack lost no time in getting down to business. He called a meeting his first morning in office, January 21, 1961. He was waiting in the Oval Office when Presidential Aide Ted Sorensen, Special Assistant Arthur Schlesinger, Jr., Press Secretary Pierre Salinger, Appointments Secretary Kenny O'Donnell, Larry O'Brien, and Dave Powers arrived. Larry O'Brien was Jack's contact with the House and Senate regarding legislation. Dave Powers was Jack's personal aide. Most of Dave's duties would be unofficial, such as swimming with the president daily, going with him to football and baseball games, and telling him funny stories. Dave's duties lightened the tension of being chief executive of the most powerful nation on earth.

Many problems faced the new president. Advances in technology were putting many people out of work. Machines did the work of many people, faster and cheaper. One out of every sixteen workers in the country was unemployed. Fewer high school and college students were finding jobs. It would take study, planning, and cooperation to work out training programs in new and different kinds of work.

Jack often substituted executive orders (acts or regulations initiated by the president) for legislation that would not pass or would be slow to pass in Congress. He felt that some problems were too important for help to be delayed or blocked by political maneuvering.

Jack was concerned about the poor and hungry of all races. On his first working day as president, he signed an executive order doubling the amount of government surplus food distributed to millions of jobless Americans and their families. Jack knew that distributing food was not the answer to hunger and poverty. It was only a short-term measure until more lasting remedies could be found. He also expanded the Food for Peace program to help starving people in other countries. On January 30 he asked Congress to include health insurance in the Social Security program. The health insurance plan was called Medicare in the bill (legislation) he sent to Congress. Although he worked hard to get the Medicare bill passed, it was defeated 52-48 in the Senate. (A similar bill was eventually passed by Congress and signed by President Lyndon Johnson in July 1965.)

Jack was always very interested in the welfare of young people. He started the President's Council on Physical Fitness, a program to encourage boys and girls to keep fit and healthy. Soon not only young people but people of every age were out jogging every day to improve their fitness and well-being.

In Mali, a country in western Africa, a Peace Corps volunteer in native costume (center) *stops to listen to one of the women with whom she works.*

One of President Kennedy's favorite projects was the Peace Corps. He set up the Peace Corps by executive order, and on March 1, 1961, he sent a message to Congress requesting legislation to make it official and to allocate, or set aside, money to pay for it. Recruitment and training of volunteers began that same spring. On September 22, 1961, Congress officially established the Peace Corps. Its purpose was to promote world peace and friendship. Volunteers were mostly young people who wanted to share their skills and energy with the people of poor nations. Peace Corps volunteers did not take part in diplomacy or intelligence (information gathering). They were teachers, doctors, nurses, carpenters, farmers, construction workers, engineers, technicians—people with many different talents. They taught school, built roads, bridges, schools, and health centers, developed farming skills—whatever was most needed. Their job was to help people in underdeveloped lands help themselves.

The Peace Corps gave people in South America, Central America, Africa, Asia, and the Near and Far East a wholly new idea of the United States and its citizens. Peace Corps volunteers were not rich Americans riding around in big cars, as most people in other countries imagined Americans to be. Volunteers lived and worked under the same conditions as the people around them. They learned and spoke the language of the people they were working with, and they went only to countries where they were invited. Peace Corps volunteers really cared about helping people, and they liked what they were doing. David Crozier, a Peace Corps volunteer in Colombia, wrote to his parents, "Should it come to it, I had rather give my life trying to help someone than to have to give my life looking down a gun barrel at them."

Judy Smith was one of the first Peace Corps volunteers to finish a two-year tour of duty in Ghion, Ethiopia, as a teacher. There, six young Americans taught 1,000 students English, music, geography, chemistry, mathematics, and health. One-third of the native students had trachoma, a serious disease of the eye .

The Peace Corps began with 500 volunteers. A year and a half later, nearly 5,000 Peace Corps volunteers were working in 45 countries around the world. The foreign minister of Thailand called the Peace Corps "this important idea, the most powerful idea in recent times. . . ." He expressed surprise that such an idea

> should come from the mightiest nation on earth, the United States. Many of us who did not know about the United States thought of this great nation as a wealthy nation, a powerful nation . . . with great material strength and many powerful weapons. But how many of us know that in the United States ideas and ideals are also powerful?

Not all of President Kennedy's undertakings met with such success. A coalition (or alliance) of Southern Democrats and Republican conservatives blocked every civil rights bill in Congress. Those two groups often voted together to block legislation they thought too liberal. Until 1954, when the Supreme Court ordered the desegregation of public schools, the separation of the races was common practice. In the South, it was often the law, and Southern congressmen did not want things to change. Many white people throughout the country also resisted changes in the civil rights of blacks.

Jack at first carried out his civil rights plan by executive order. He was aware of the unjust treatment of black people in the United States, especially in the South. He wanted not only to eliminate discrimination, but also to teach people that discrimination was wrong. As a congressman and senator, Jack had voted for every civil rights bill that had been introduced. In his first debate with Richard Nixon during the presidential campaign, he had said:

> The Negro baby born in America today...has about one-half as much chance of completing high school as a white baby...one-third as much chance of completing college...twice as much chance of becoming unemployed...a life expectancy which is seven years shorter, and the prospects of earning only one-half as much.

The civil rights movement was in full swing when Jack took office. Under the leadership of Martin Luther King, Jr., blacks—joined by many Northern whites—were nonviolently protesting against segregated public facilities (restaurants, stores, schools) and unjust treatment.

In 1961 Freedom Riders rode buses to different Southern towns and cities to desegregate public facilities. Freedom

Civil rights workers endured many forms of violence, including attacks by police dogs.

Riders were mostly young people, both black and white, from many parts of the United States. In May the Freedom Riders planned to go by bus from Nashville, Tennessee, to Montgomery, Alabama. John Seigenthaler was sent by President Kennedy to ride the bus and observe the situation. The bus was met in Montgomery by a wild mob, and the Freedom Riders were attacked. Seigenthaler was beaten until he was unconscious while the police stood and watched.

This was just one of a number of similar incidents all over the South. While King was addressing a group of 1,200 people in a Montgomery church, a mob of 3,000 to 4,000 angry whites surrounded the building. Martin Luther King called Attorney General Bobby Kennedy to ask for protection

James Meredith was the first black person to enroll at the University of Mississippi.

for the people inside the church. Bobby ordered 600 federal marshals to the scene to restore order, and he called Governor John Patterson. Bobby told the governor that if he did not provide additional protection for the people inside the church, President Kennedy would send in the National Guard and take care of the problem himself. The governor called about 300 troops. The federal marshals broke up the crowd with tear gas.

After being inspired by President Kennedy's inaugural address, a black air force veteran, James Meredith, applied for admission to the University of Mississippi. On September 20, when Meredith appeared at the university in Oxford, he found the doorway blocked by the governor of Mississippi, Ross Barnett. Although Bobby Kennedy had sent 200 federal marshals to see that Meredith was safely admitted, the governor and a group of state troopers—backed by an ever-growing mob—turned Meredith and the troops away. For the next several days Meredith tried again and again to gain admission to the school. Court rulings ordered his admission, but Governor Barnett and the university defied the rulings.

On Saturday, September 29, the president became involved and called the governor himself. "I have to carry out the Constitution of the United States. I need your help in doing it," he told the governor. Barnett proposed a plan to quietly enroll Meredith on Sunday, when few people would be on campus.

Unwilling to rely on Governor Barnett's word, Jack federalized the National Guard. He also ordered more federal troops to a base in Memphis, Tennessee, about 60 miles (97 kilometers) from Oxford, Mississippi. On Sunday, September 30, instead of being quietly admitted, James Meredith was met at the school by a crowd of 2,500 angry whites, some armed with shotguns and rifles.

The governor had withdrawn all state troops, and the 200 federal marshals whom Bobby had called in were no match for the enraged mob. The mob began attacking the federal marshals with rocks, pipes, clubs, bricks, firebombs, and guns. Deputy Attorney General Nicholas Katzenbach ordered the marshals to respond with tear gas, but to keep their pistols in their holsters. Hundreds of people were injured, two were killed.

Meanwhile, believing that the admission of Meredith was going smoothly, as Governor Barnett assured him it would, President Kennedy was making a television address to the nation. He said,

> Our nation is founded on the principle that observance
> of the law is the eternal safeguard of liberty. . . . Even

President Kennedy personally told Governor Ross Barnett of Mississippi to obey the law and the Constitution of the United States.

among law-abiding men, few laws are universally loved, but they are uniformly respected and not resisted. Americans are free to disagree with the law, but not to disobey it. For in a government of laws and not of men, no man, however prominent and powerful, and no mob, however unruly or boisterous, is entitled to defy a court of law. . . .

After the speech, Jack was heartsick and angry when he was told what was happening in Mississippi. He called Governor Barnett and demanded that the governor and the university comply with the Constitution and the law. When the governor still argued, Jack hung up in disgust. Then the governor called back and said he would recall the National Guard and the local police.

The president sent additional federal troops, and the violence finally died down early on Monday morning. Meredith, accompanied by a group of marshals, was quietly enrolled as a student at the University of Mississippi.

Bobby and Jack had always worked closely together, and they continued to do so during the civil rights struggle. It was Bobby and other Department of Justice officials who carried out quiet meetings with school boards in Atlanta, Dallas, Memphis, New Orleans, and other cities. As a result, many schools were integrated with a minimum of fuss. Railroads, bus stations, and airlines followed a similar pattern.

Although the president could not persuade Congress to pass the civil rights laws he wanted, he used litigation (lawsuits), negotiation, persuasion, executive orders, directives, and personal actions as powerful tools in the cause of civil rights. Jack publicly endorsed the principle of equal rights, and he was able to force many small but significant changes in policy that set a whole new tone.

For example, Jack directed people in his administration to refuse to speak before segregated audiences, and they were directed to boycott segregated private clubs. U.S. employment offices were told to refuse job orders "for whites only." When Jack spoke at press club dinners, black faces were among the formerly all-white audience. Black as well as white members of the Secret Service guarded the president, and blacks were included in the pool of White House drivers.

On June 11, 1963, the president decided to address the nation about civil rights. He committed himself and the country "to the proposition that race has no place in American life or law." He talked about legislation he would send to Congress, but he also said that "legislation cannot solve the problem alone. It must be solved in the homes of every American." He pointed out the moral injustice of racial discrimination. "We are confronted primarily with a moral issue.... Now the time has come for this nation to fulfill its promise.... Those who do nothing are inviting shame as well as violence. Those who act boldly are recognizing right as well as reality."

On June 19 the president sent to Congress the broadest civil rights bill ever proposed. In his message he said that simple justice required this program "not merely for reasons of economic efficiency, world diplomacy and domestic tranquility — but, above all, because it is right."

On August 28, 1963, a singular event took place: the historic March on Washington. People, both blacks and whites, from all over the country, 250,000 strong, marched from the Washington Monument to the Lincoln Memorial. It was the largest public demonstration that had ever been held in Washington. People marveled at the spirit and self-discipline of the marchers. The crowd was quiet and orderly. Many listened with tears in their eyes as they heard Martin Luther King's ringing words: "I have a dream that my four little children will one day live in a nation where they will be judged not by the color of their skin, but by the content of their character.... I have a dream," he cried again and again, describing the day when peace and equality would prevail.

> When we let freedom ring, when we let it ring from every village and every hamlet, from every state and every city, we will be able to speed up that day when all God's children, black and white....Jews and Gentiles, Protestants and Catholics, will be able to join in the words of that old Negro spiritual,"Free at last! Free at last! Thank God Almighty, we are free at last!"

"I have a dream," Martin Luther King *told the 250,000 people gathered for the* March on Washington. *His words renewed people's hope.*

Leaders of the March on Washington pose for pictures with President Kennedy. Vice President Johnson and Secretary of Labor Willard Wirtz stand to the right of the president. Martin Luther King is third from the left.

After the march, several prominent black leaders were invited to the White House to talk to the president. Jack met them and led them to his private quarters. When Jack learned that most of them hadn't had a chance to eat all day, he had food brought in. They discussed with Jack ways to bring about the reforms they so badly needed. When they left, they felt that Jack Kennedy was a strong fighter on their side.

On a trip to Mexico (top), *the people greeted President Kennedy's motorcade with red, white, and blue confetti. Crowds were equally enthusiastic when he visited Venezuela and Colombia in 1962* (bottom).

◇ EIGHT ◇

Foreign Policy

1961-1962

One of Jack Kennedy's worst failures happened shortly after he took office. The large island of Cuba, just 90 miles (145 km) south of Florida, had fallen into communist hands in 1959, when Fidel Castro and a band of rebels overthrew the government of dictator Fulgencio Batista. Under Castro's leadership, Cuba became a communist country. Its government allows only one political party—the Cuban Communist Party.

After World War II, the American government and many private citizens became worried about communism. They viewed it as a threat to their democratic way of life. The United States government was very concerned about having a communist neighbor, so some government officials decided to mount an attack on Castro's forces. The plan would use 1,400 Cuban exiles, called the Cuban Brigade. The exiles had been trained by the U.S. military in Guatemala.

The CIA, which was in charge of this plan, had bought some old World War II B-26 bombers and freighters. The Bay of Pigs in Cuba was to be the landing place. The whole action was to be the work of the Cubans themselves. It was thought that, once the Cuban Brigade had landed, the Cuban people would rise up in revolt and support the invaders.

When former President Eisenhower first told Jack of the plan, Jack was appalled. He had never expected to be met with a situation like this in his first month in office. He discussed the plan with his brother-in-law Steve Smith and with Bobby. He told them, "It just doesn't feel right."

Jack lost no time in calling a meeting of his advisers. Allen Dulles and Richard Bissel, both of the CIA, General Lemnitzer, chairman of the Joint Chiefs of Staff, and Admiral Arleigh Burke, chief of naval operations, all advised Jack to go ahead with the plan.

Jack had his doubts. Other members of his staff also felt unsure about the wisdom of the plan, but they didn't speak out very forcefully. Dulles and Bissel urged haste and secrecy. Jack reluctantly gave his consent.

On Sunday, April 17, 1961, the invasion began. The planners were not familiar with conditions at the Bay of Pigs. The invasion became an incredible series of blunders based on faulty information about Castro's military strength.

Two freighters carrying ammunition, communication equipment, and food and medical supplies were sunk by Castro's small air force, and half of the B-26s were shot down. Supplies never reached the Cuban exiles on the beach. Because he wasn't informed of its military importance, Jack canceled a second air strike that might have provided cover for the invasion. Jack had approved a plan that didn't even resemble what he thought he'd approved.

The Cuban underground, a secret group in Cuba that was supposed to have rallied the Cuban people to support the invaders, never knew about the plan. Without supplies, ammunition, arms, or air cover, Cuban Brigade 2506 fought on bravely until they were killed or captured.

Jack felt terrible about the whole affair. "How could I have been so stupid," he asked, "to let them go ahead?" The doomed venture came to an end on Wednesday. There had been many shocking errors in the decision-making process. Although it had been an Eisenhower project that Jack had inherited, he refused to let anyone in his administration make excuses for him. "As chief executive, it was my responsibility," he said. He did learn a lesson from the experience. From then on, he made sure to examine all sides of a question, and he never again made a decision hastily.

There were many other pressing problems that required Jack's attention. One of them was the matter of how to deal with Soviet Premier Nikita Khrushchev. Khrushchev thought that Jack was too young to be taken seriously as a head of state. Jack thought that the Russian leader was rude, shrewd, cunning, and obstinate. Khrushchev invited President Kennedy to meet with him in Vienna, Austria, in early June 1961. Kennedy wanted to meet Khrushchev so that they might understand each other better. Jacqueline accompanied her husband to Europe. Nikita was charmed by Jacqueline, but he and Jack could not come to a meeting of the minds. They faced the problem of two great nations with different social systems trying to avoid head-on collision. Two important points of disagreement hinged on the requirements for a nuclear test ban treaty (an agreement to stop tests of nuclear weapons) and the presence of Western troops in Berlin.

Kennedy met with Nikita Khrushchev in Vienna, Austria, in 1961.

At the end of World War II, control of Germany had been divided into sectors controlled by the Allied forces: England, France, the Soviet Union, and the United States. The city of Berlin, the capital of Germany at that time, was located in what became the Soviet zone. But because the city was so important, it too was divided into sectors. The Soviets controlled East Berlin. West Berlin was under the control of Britain, France, and the United States. Military troops stayed there to protect and maintain the established sectors, or zones.

Khrushchev wanted all but the Soviet troops out of Berlin. But leaving would have meant abandoning about 2 million West Berliners, allowing them to fall under East German communist control. President Kennedy refused to do that.

Also, the Soviet Union would not agree to inspection of its nuclear test sites. Without inspection, the United States

*The Kennedys attended the Paris Opera with French President
Charles de Gaulle,* center.

would have no way of knowing whether or not the Soviet
Union was obeying the rules of the treaty.

The two leaders did come to a tentative agreement on
other issues, and they made a joint statement promising to
keep in contact with each other. They may also have learned
to like each other a little bit and to appreciate each other's
differences.

One day at lunch during the meetings in Vienna, Jack
noticed that Khrushchev was wearing a large medal. Jack
asked what it was.

"The Lenin Peace Medal," Khrushchev replied.

"I hope you are planning to keep it," the president said
with a smile.

Before going to Austria, Jack and Jacqueline had visited Charles de Gaulle, the tall, dignified president of France. France wanted to develop its own atomic bomb. Jack hoped to persuade President de Gaulle that the fewer nations who had the bomb, the safer all nations would be.

While the two presidents may have had some disagreements, Paris went wild over Jacqueline Kennedy. She was of French descent and spoke French fluently. Her passion for the arts and her flawless style charmed the skeptical Parisians. The crowds greeting them shouted "Jacqui! Jacqui!" (JA-key). Jack jokingly described himself as "the man who accompanied Jacqueline Kennedy to Paris." De Gaulle also was charmed by Jacqueline's beauty and intelligence, and he was flattered by Jack's obvious respect. De Gaulle still believed, however, that France should develop its own nuclear bomb.

The Kennedys also stopped in Great Britain. Jack met with British Prime Minister Harold Macmillan. He also paid his first and only visit to the grave of his beloved "Kicks," his sister Kathleen, who had been killed in an airplane accident over France and had been buried in Britain.

On Tuesday morning, October 16, 1962, Jack—still in his robe—was having breakfast in his room when McGeorge Bundy, his national security adviser, called on him. What Bundy had to tell him was shocking. The U.S. government had photos showing that the Soviet Union was building a missile base in Cuba!

For months Soviet ships had been delivering mysterious equipment to Cuba. When asked about this, Anatoly Dobrynin, Soviet ambassador to the United States, had said that the Soviets were only sending defensive weapons and equipment

MRBM LAUNCH SITE 3
SAN CRISTOBAL, CUBA
27 OCTOBER 1962

LAUNCH AREA

NUCLEAR WARHEAD BUNKER U/C

PERMANENT BLDGS

OPEN STORAGE

This aerial photo shows one of the missile sites in Cuba, located about 100 miles from Florida.

in case the United States attacked Cuba. However, photos taken by U.S. reconnaissance planes showed missile sites close to completion.

Jack was outwardly calm and cool, but privately he was furious with Khrushchev for deceiving him. He quickly set up a meeting of top officials and trusted friends and advisers. The group became known as the Executive Committee. The press dubbed it ExCom. John McCone, head of the CIA, Attorney General Robert Kennedy, Defense Secretary Robert McNamara, Secretary of State Dean Rusk, Treasury Secretary Douglas Dillon, United Nations Ambassador Adlai Stevenson, General Maxwell Taylor, McGeorge Bundy, Ted Sorensen,

The Executive Committee (above) *met frequently as events unfolded during the missile crisis. The members often disagreed about what action to take, if any. Bobby Kennedy is at far left. Jack confers privately with Bobby,* below.

and Vice President Johnson were among those who made up the committee.

Each day brought more evidence against the Soviets. The members of the committee were sharply divided in their opinions about what should be done. Some wanted immediate bombing of the missile sites and invasion of Cuba. Jack and Bobby felt that this action would bring on an all-out nuclear war. Others thought that a naval blockade of Cuban shores might stop the construction of the missile base. Bobby and McNamara favored this approach, and that was the course of action Jack decided to follow.

On Monday, October 22, President Kennedy spoke to the American people on television. He told them exactly what was happening. The whole nation was very concerned. Jack asked Jacqueline if she wanted to take the children away from Washington, which would probably be the first target of an attack. Jacqueline said no, she wanted to stay with Jack.

The week dragged on with the Executive Committee meeting at all hours of the day and night. Messages flew back and forth between Khrushchev and Kennedy. The messages from Khrushchev were confusing. Sometimes he seemed to be proposing peace. Other times he was blustering and warlike. It was hard to tell what he really meant. Meanwhile, 18 Soviet cargo ships had been spotted steaming toward Cuba, and Soviet submarines had been sent to protect them.

The president sent a message to Khrushchev demanding that the ships turn back, and that missile bases and missiles be removed from Cuba. Jack said the U.S. Navy was prepared to halt, board, and confiscate the Soviet ships if they kept on their course to Cuba. Jack also demanded that the Soviet submarines turn back.

The USS *Joseph P. Kennedy* was among the destroyers taking part in the sea blockade near Cuba. One Lebanese freighter, which had been chartered by the Soviet Union, was boarded and then allowed to pass. The cargo ships and their submarine escort drew closer. Finally, they stopped to await further orders. At the end of the week the Soviet vessels turned and went back toward their homeland. Khrushchev had evidently given the order. U.S. planes followed them back to their Soviet ports.

On Friday evening, October 26, the president received a message from Khrushchev that hinted at an agreement. The message was vague, but Khrushchev seemed to be saying that he would withdraw the missiles if the United States would promise not to invade Cuba. While the ExCom was meeting on Saturday, Khrushchev sent another message that contradicted Friday's message. Then the committee learned that a U.S. reconnaissance plane had been shot down over Cuba and another Soviet ship was approaching the blockade.

Jack decided to act as though Khrushchev had offered a settlement and to ignore the Soviet leader's latest statement. The president sent a letter, written with the help of the committee, in which he said the United States would accept the Soviet offer to remove the missiles from Cuba under United Nations supervision. In return, the United States promised not to invade Cuba and to halt the blockade. Everyone in ExCom and the rest of the government waited tensely for the reply. The peace of the world hung in the balance.

Finally a message came from the Soviet premier in a telegram: "The Soviet government has ordered the dismantling of bases and dispatching of equipment from the USSR... I appreciate your assurance that the United States will not invade Cuba. Nikita Khrushchev."

In March 1961 Jack initiated the Alliance for Progress to help form stronger ties between the United States and South and Central America. Most of the countries of South America were ruled by dictators. The people had no voice in government. Wealthy landowners lived in luxury; the rest of the population lived in misery. Much the same conditions existed in Central America. Jack wanted to do something to relieve the poverty of the people and to reform their dictatorial systems.

Jack and Jacqueline went to Venezuela and Colombia in December of 1961. Just three years before, crowds in Lima, Peru, and Caracas, Venezuela, had thrown stones at and spit on Vice President Richard Nixon and his wife. Although authorities feared more anti-American demonstrations and even violence, their fears were unfounded. Everywhere they went, the Kennedys were greeted by cheering crowds. In Bogotá, Colombia, Jack outlined a plan for democratic reform, economic development, and a united front against poverty and oppression. He pledged United States aid to "make of this hemisphere a bright and shining light." In an open field near Bogotá, Jack dedicated a future *Alianza* housing project. A year later he received a grateful letter from the first family to move into the project. It was the first time the family had had a permanent home, and it had given them a "sense of dignity," the letter stated. Jack hoped the Peace Corps volunteers would help with the Alliance for Progress, and they did, but much more help was needed.

The president seemed to be more amused than scared when Caroline (left) and John, Jr. began trick-or-treating in the Oval Office.

◇ NINE ◇

Life at the White House
1961-1963

The Kennedys had scarcely arrived home when they got very bad news. Joseph Kennedy had suffered a massive stroke and was paralyzed. Jacqueline Kennedy felt almost as sad as Jack did at the tragedy. She had become very fond of her father-in-law. Jack was stunned. He had always been very close to his father, even though they often had differing opinions. Joseph Kennedy was unable to talk, although his mind was clear. He lived for eight more years, but he was never able to walk again. One bright spot for all the Kennedys was that Teddy, the youngest son, was elected to the U.S. Senate in November 1962.

In spite of being a very busy president, Jack Kennedy found time to romp with his children. One of John, Jr.'s favorite games was one he made up himself. He would hide behind the movable panel in his father's desk. Jack had to rap on

Caroline and John, Jr., often paid surprise visits to their father.

the panel and ask, "Is the bunny home?" John, Jr., would jump out, a delighted smile on his face, while his father acted surprised. The little boy also went swimming with Jack and Dave Powers in the White House swimming pool.

Both Caroline and John, Jr., often burst in on their father in the morning, while he was eating breakfast in his bedroom. They had things to show him or tell him. Jack usually listened with great attention—sometimes to an imaginary adventure of John, Jr.'s. At other times Jack and Caroline had serious discussions about Caroline's pony, Macaroni.

Jack was usually in his office by 9:00 A.M. Often his busy day was brightened by glimpses of his children play-ing. Sometimes Caroline popped into a meeting dressed in her mother's high heels. John, Jr., could be seen waving a tiny American flag while marching up and down a White House balcony.

Jack and Caroline chat as she rides Macaroni. Below, Caroline and friends raid the candy jar of the president's secretary. Jack limits their take to one piece each.

Top, *the Kennedys talk with composer Igor Stravinsky and his wife, Vera.* Below, *at a reception of Nobel Prize winners, Jack talks with writer Pearl Buck while Jacqueline listens to poet Robert Frost.*

Jacqueline asked the people of the United States to help her find antiques that might once have been part of the White House furnishings. She wanted to restore the mansion to its former charm and dignity. She herself had found a priceless antique desk and other items of historical interest in a basement storeroom of the White House. People responded from all over the land.

There was a big change in life-style at the White House when the Kennedys moved in. White House dinners became occasions at which wit, culture, and sparkling intellect were the order of the evening. Jack and Jacqueline were gracious hosts, and they set the pace for lively discussions. At one dinner in honor of Nobel Prize winners, Jack said, "I think this is the most extraordinary collection of talent, of human knowledge, that has ever been gathered together at the White House—with the possible exception of when Thomas Jefferson dined alone."

Jack (center, on platform) *was appalled by the sight of the Berlin Wall, separating what was then East Berlin from West Berlin. Below, the president signs the Nuclear Test Ban Treaty.*

◊ TEN ◊

Reaching for
Peace and Freedom

1961-1963

The Soviets had launched a space capsule, *Sputnik I*, into orbit around the Earth in 1957. In 1961 Soviet cosmonaut Yuri Gagarin became the first person to orbit the Earth.

When Jack became president, he decided that the United States should catch up with the Soviet Union in the field of space development. He said, "We have vowed that we shall see space filled not with weapons of mass destruction, but with instruments of knowledge and understanding." Jack's goal was to land a person on the Moon by the end of the century. To accomplish this ambitious goal, the United States used the best scientific minds the country had to offer. Scientists had to develop a booster rocket powerful enough to overcome the pull of the Earth's gravity and send a spacecraft into orbit.

People at NASA (the National Aeronautics and Space Administration) tried many different types of rocket launchers and rockets. Finally they developed an Atlas rocket powerful enough to carry a man into space. Lieutenant Commander Alan Shepard became the first American to make a space flight in May 1961. On February 20, 1962, John Glenn circled the Earth three times. He was the first American to orbit the Earth.

Glenn's physical condition was excellent when he returned to Earth, and he brought back much valuable information. Later, New York welcomed Glenn and President Kennedy with a ticker-tape parade.

The second U.S. piloted space flight took place on May 24, 1962, when Lieutenant Scott Carpenter orbited the Earth three times in *Aurora 7*.

Between October 4, 1961, and October 3, 1962, the United States placed 46 satellites in orbit and launched 4 space probes. Some were launched to do basic research about space and piloted flight. Others were concerned with weather, communications, and navigation. One of the probes, *Mariner II*, came close enough to Venus to take photos of that planet. Ranger Moon probes sent back detailed photos of the Moon's surface. Tyros weather satellites provided clear pictures of the Earth's surface and atmosphere. With the information from the Tyros, meteorologists could accurately predict storms, hurricanes, and other weather conditions. With each step, research was bringing human beings closer to the Moon.

As John Kennedy said, "The eyes of the world now look into space, to the Moon, and to the planets beyond, and we have vowed that we shall see space governed not by a hostile flag of conquest, but by a banner of freedom and peace." During this period, the Soviet Union and the United States were competing with each other in space development. Each

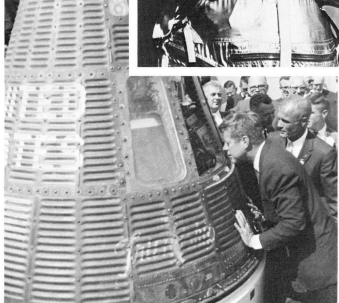

Astronaut John Glenn (top and also to the president's right, bottom photo), *who orbited the Earth three times, explains to Jack how the space capsule works.*

President Kennedy spoke to thousands of cheering West Berliners when he visited the city in June 1963.

country's leadership in science, engineering, and national defense was measured to a great degree by its success in space.

Between the end of World War II in 1945 and the summer of 1961, about 3.5 million East Germans had left their homes and jobs to gain their freedom in West Berlin. Most East Germans fled through Berlin, because the communist East German government had sealed off the border between East and West Germany. Over 30,000 East Germans had fled in July 1961 alone. They could not help noticing the freedom and relative wealth of West Berliners compared to their own way of life. The mass departure dramatized to the whole world the failure of the communist system. In August 1961, Khrushchev's response to this outpouring was to construct the Berlin Wall — a barrier of concrete and barbed wire cutting through the heart of Berlin and dividing the city. East Germans could not get out and West Germans could not get in. By building the wall, East Germans shocked the free world.

When President Kennedy visited West Germany in June 1963, the wall was still there. Jack was appalled at his first sight of it—grim, gray, and forbidding. It kept apart German families, friends, and neighbors. Jack spoke to a huge crowd that filled the city square and streets in every direction. Jack told them:

> Today, in the world of freedom, the proudest boast is "Ich bin ein Berliner." There are many people in the world today who really don't understand, or say they don't, what is the great issue between the free world and the communist world. Let—them—come —to—Berlin!... All free men, wherever they may live, are citizens of Berlin, and therefore, as a free man, I take pride in the words, "Ich bin ein Berliner!" [I am a Berliner!]

"Ken-ne-dy! Ken-ne-dy!" the crowd chanted. There was no longer any doubt in the minds of the German people. They felt sure of the friendship of the United States.

From Berlin Kennedy went to Dublin, Ireland, the home of his ancestors. The people there treated him like a long lost son. Dave Powers said the reception Jack received along stately O'Connell Street was more enthusiastic than a St. Patrick's Day parade in South Boston and a Bunker Hill parade in Charlestown put together.

After Dublin, Jack and his entourage traveled through the misty green countryside to Dunganstown in County Wexford. This was where Jack's great-grandfather, Patrick Kennedy, had been born. Jack's cousin, Mrs. Mary Ryan,

In Dunganstown in County Wexford, Ireland, Jack visited his Fitz-gerald and his Kennedy relatives.

whom Jack had visited once before, laid out a fine party in her yard. Every relative for miles around was an honored guest. On a long table set with a fine Irish linen cloth was a feast, with slabs of ham, Galway salmon, cheese, homemade soda bread, tea, scones (biscuits), and cake. After the party, Jack left for New Ross, Ireland.

It was from New Ross that Jack's great-grandfather had left for America. The people in New Ross presented Jack with a beautiful gold box. On the cover was the Kennedy coat of arms, and around the border was the Fitzgerald clan insignia.

Jack thanked them for the beautiful gift, then went on, with a glint of humor in his eyes, "If Great-Grandfather Kennedy hadn't come to America, I might be working at the fertilizer company across the street."

Jack's evident enjoyment and his ready Irish wit won their affection. Jack looked around at his relatives: the black-haired, blue-eyed "black Irish"—the Fitzgerald side of the family—and the red-haired, freckle-faced, blue-eyed Kennedys, whose looks he had inherited. "I'm glad to see," he remarked, "a few of the cousins who didn't catch the boat."

Jack returned from his successful tour with the admiration and trust of the German people and with the hearts of the Irish in his keeping.

One of the first things Jack wanted to do when he returned to Washington was to negotiate a nuclear test ban treaty with the Soviet Union. He had laid the groundwork for the treaty when he met with Khrushchev. Now Jack bent all his efforts toward achieving his goal.

Finally, after months of quiet talks with the Soviets, Jack's efforts began to bear fruit. In January 1963, Jack had postponed nuclear tests in Nevada to show that the United States wanted a test ban treaty. The Soviets also indicated that they might be interested in banning nuclear tests.

Many meetings took place to work out the terms of the treaty. By July Great Britain, the Soviet Union, and the United States had agreed on the main points related to banning nuclear tests in the atmosphere. On July 25 representatives from the three nations initialed copies of the treaty in Moscow. Jack went on television and told the American people:

> I speak to you tonight in a spirit of hope.... [Since] the advent of nuclear weapons, all mankind has been struggling to escape from the darkening prospect of mass destruction on earth....
> Yesterday a shaft of light cut into the darkness....
> This treaty is not the millennium.... But it is

an important first step—a step toward peace, a step toward reason, a step away from war....

According to the ancient Chinese proverb, "A journey of 1000 miles must begin with a single step...". Let us take that first step.

On September 24, 1963, the U.S. Senate approved, or ratified, the Nuclear Test Ban Treaty, and it became effective for all three countries on October 10.

As he signed the treaty, Jack said, "The age of nuclear energy has been full of fear, yet never empty of hope. Today the fear is a little less and the hope is a little greater....I hereby pledge, on behalf of the United States, if this treaty fails it will not be our doing."

The Test Ban Treaty may have been John Kennedy's crowning achievement. But he still had many serious problems. One of the most serious was the conflict in Vietnam, in Southeast Asia.

In 1954 Vietnam had been divided into North Vietnam and South Vietnam by an international conference. The purpose of the conference was to arrange a peace settlement after France was defeated in its attempt to rule Vietnam. The settlement also called for an election in 1956 to unite Vietnam under one government.

North Vietnam was communist-controlled. Its leader was Premier Ho Chi Minh, who had led a revolutionary group, called the *Vietminh*, in the fight for independence from French rule. Ho Chi Minh was strongly allied with communist China. In 1955 Ngo Dinh Diem was chosen as the leader of South Vietnam. Diem's government was harsh. Claiming the Communist Party would not permit fair elections, Diem refused to allow the 1956 election to take place. His continued oppression and indifference to the needs of his people caused a virtual civil war. One group of Vietnamese people supported President Diem. Another group, members of the Vietminh, later called Viet Cong, supported Ho Chi Minh. The latter group wanted all of Vietnam united under Ho Chi Minh's leadership. The Viet Cong were trained in guerrilla warfare by communist North Vietnam, which was aided by communist China.

While Eisenhower was still president, South Vietnam had asked the United States for help in fighting the guerrilla raids by the Viet Cong. Guerrilla warfare consists of striking quick blows from an ambush and then disappearing into the trackless jungle or countryside. It was difficult for soldiers trained in conventional methods of warfare, as Diem's army was, to fight against this kind of attack.

President Eisenhower had sent supplies and military advisers to help train the South Vietnamese army. Jack was left with this commitment when he became president. Late in 1961, he sent more advisers as well as helicopters and supplies.

Although the United States kept sending more people and more supplies every year, the Viet Cong showed no signs of backing down. At the same time, the war itself was creating a serious division among people in the United States. Many viewed it as a civil war that had to be decided by the Vietnamese people themselves—without another country interfering.

Jack told his brother Bobby that, after the upcoming election in 1964, his first priority would be to get the United States out of Vietnam. He had come to believe that the war in Vietnam was a political struggle within that country, and that the United States had no real reason to be there. In May 1963, President Kennedy asked the Pentagon, which is the

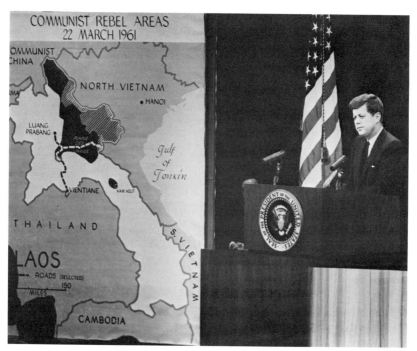

Kennedy wanted to withdraw U.S. troops from Vietnam after the '64 election.

U.S. Defense Department headquarters, to draw up a schedule to phase out all U.S. involvement in Vietnam by the end of 1965. With typical Kennedy confidence, Jack had no doubt that he would win the coming election in 1964.

In August 1963, Jacqueline gave birth to a baby son, Patrick. Patrick died, shortly after birth, of a breathing difficulty. Both Jack and Jacqueline were grief-stricken. Caroline and John had been promised a baby brother, and they were disappointed.

The president's busy schedule went on, filled with meetings, speeches, and press conferences. Jack was good at ad-libbing, although he was usually well informed about most

Jack's keen wit and intelligence helped him during press conferences.

issues and could anticipate reporters' questions. When he was asked an unexpected question, his witty answers usually got him out of difficulties and delighted his audience.

The upcoming election in 1964 was on Jack's mind. As it drew nearer, Jack looked to Vice President Johnson for help in Johnson's home state of Texas. The Democrats in Texas were bitterly divided into two camps: supporters of conservative Governor John Connally and supporters of the more liberal Senator Ralph Yarborough. Texas was too important a state to lose, and if the Democrats were fighting among themselves, it might be easy for a Republican candidate to win. Jack thought visiting Texas with Vice President Johnson might help to heal the breach.

◇ ELE

The Legacy
1963

John Kennedy knew that a segment of the population in Texas did not approve of his stand on civil rights. But Jack was sure that differences of opinion could be solved through reason and goodwill. He was, in fact, planning to talk about reason and goodwill in his speech at a luncheon at the Dallas, Texas, trade mart. During the flight to Dallas, Jack put finishing touches on the speech. The concluding paragraph read:

> We ... in this generation, are — by destiny rather than by choice — the watchmen on the walls of freedom. We ask therefore ... that we may exercise our strength with wisdom and restraint — and that we may achieve in our time and for all time the ancient vision of 'peace on earth, goodwill toward men.' That must always be our goal. ...

Jacqueline accompanied her husband to Texas. Their first stop on November 21 was in San Antonio, where many were of Mexican descent. Jack had been invited a new aerospace medical center there. The way e airport to the center was lined with cheering, usiastic people. They threw handfuls of colorful con-tti and carried hand-lettered signs saying *BIENVENIDO* (WELCOME) MR. PRESIDENT AND JACKIE. Jacqueline enjoyed the welcome as much as Jack, and she spoke to the delighted people in perfect Spanish.

The presidential party flew from San Antonio to Houston, and then on to Fort Worth, where they were to spend the night. Although there were scattered signs in both cities saying things like, BAN THE BROTHERS and KENNEDY, KHRUSHCHEV, AND KING, and editorials in the news-papers calling the president a traitor, crowds for the most part were friendly.

On the morning of November 22, Jack met in the hotel parking lot with some of the "ordinary" people of Fort Worth—mechanics, truck drivers, secretaries, clerks, housewives—who, Jack said, were his true constituents. Later he and Jacqueline were to be the luncheon guests of the Fort Worth Chamber of Commerce. When Jacqueline appeared in the hotel dining room, beautiful in a pink suit and a matching hat, there was an audible stir of admiration. Reporters gathered around her. The president, delighted, quipped, "Why is it no one cares what Lyndon and I wear?"

It was a short plane hop from Fort Worth to Dallas. When their plane landed at Love Field, the president and Jacqueline received an ovation. People kept pushing their hands through the airport fence to try to touch the president or shake his hand. The mayor's wife presented Jacqueline with a bouquet of red roses.

Jack responded to a constituent in Fort Worth, Texas, top. *When the Kennedys arrived in Dallas, Jacqueline received a bouquet of roses,* bottom.

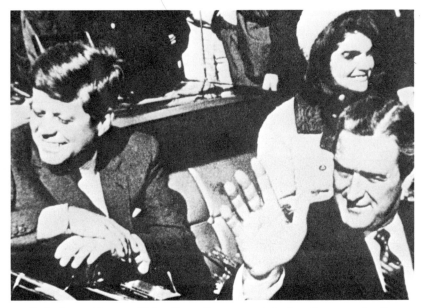

Jack, Jacqueline, and John Connally moments before the assassination

Because they were concerned about the president's safety, the Secret Service had shipped a bubble-top car to Dallas for the president's use. The top was a removable, see-through cover that allowed spectators and occupants to see, while at the same time protecting the riders from weather or the press of the crowds. It had rained earlier, but the weather had turned warm and sunny. Jack insisted that the bubble top be removed. So far, the welcome had been warm and sincere, and there had been no threatening or hostile incidents. Fears for the president's safety had faded away.

About 250,000 people lined the streets in Dallas along the route of the presidential motorcade. As the cars approached Dealey Plaza—a wide, grass-covered area—three streets came together: Houston, Elm, and Main. The presidential car made a sharp turn north onto Elm. The Texas School Book

Depository, a dull-orange brick building, was on their right. The road dipped downhill at that point.

A Secret Service agent drove the car, and another sat next to him with a rifle close at hand. Governor and Mrs. Connally sat in front of Jacqueline and the president, who occupied the back seat. Secret Service agents also rode in a car following the presidential party.

Mrs. Connally turned around and said to the president, "You can't say Dallas wasn't friendly." At that moment a sharp, cracking sound, like an auto backfiring, pierced the air. Jacqueline, who had been waving to the people on her left, turned to face Jack. Jack's hand went to his throat and he began to fall forward. At almost the same time the governor gave a sharp cry and bent over. Both President Kennedy and John Connally had been shot. Seconds later there was another shot, and the back of the president's head was torn away.

Jacqueline saw Clint Hill, a Secret Service man, trying to climb from the street onto the back of the car. She crawled toward Mr. Hill and held out her hand to him. He scrambled in and pushed Jacqueline down. He threw himself over the president's body to shield him.

The presidential car drew out of line and raced to the nearest hospital while agents radioed ahead. Doctors and orderlies met the president's car at the entrance to Parkland Memorial Hospital. They rushed the body of the president to Trauma Room One. Governor Connally was taken to another emergency room.

Everything possible was done to save the president, but it was hopeless. Jack had no pulse, no blood pressure. John Connally's wound was serious, but not fatal.

Two priests from nearby Holy Trinity Church hurried to the hospital. They gave Jack the last rites of the Catholic

Jacqueline, right, *stood next to Johnson when he took the oath of office aboard* Air Force One.

church. Father Huber, the pastor of the church, prayed, "Eternal rest grant unto him, O Lord."

Jacqueline, who stood close, finished, "And let perpetual light shine upon him."

Vice President Johnson, not knowing if the shooting was part of a conspiracy or the act of one person, decided he should get back to Washington at once. In a short time the president's body was carried onto *Air Force One.* Jacqueline, Vice President Johnson, Mrs. Johnson, and other members of the presidential party boarded the plane for Washington.

Inside the plane Lyndon Johnson took the oath of office, administered by Judge Sarah Hughes. Lyndon Johnson became the 36th president of the United States. Jacqueline Kennedy stood, dazed and numb with shock, unmindful of her blood-stained clothes, beside the new president.

In the Rotunda of the Capitol, Jacqueline kissed the flag covering the bier and Caroline reached up to touch it—a final goodbye.

Jacqueline, Caroline, and John, Jr., leave the cathedral. Behind them, left to right, *are Peter Lawford, Bobby Kennedy, and Eunice Kennedy Shriver.*

The day after its return from Dallas, President Kennedy's body lay in its flag-draped casket, on the same bier (or stand) that had held the body of Abraham Lincoln in the Rotunda of the Capitol. All day and all evening people filed past the casket. Lines of people, six abreast, stood in bitter cold for hours, waiting for a chance to say goodbye to their president.

After the last mourner left, and the doors of the Rotunda were closed to the public, Jacqueline and Caroline slipped into the building for one last visit. They knelt before the closed casket and said some prayers. Caroline reached up and touched the flag draping the casket, as though the act could bring her father closer.

Thousands of grieving citizens lined the streets to pay their last respects as the caisson passed, carrying the body of John F. Kennedy.

John Kennedy's funeral was attended by kings, princesses and princes, presidents, prime ministers, and representatives of 92 countries from around the world, and by millions of grieving American citizens. Many lined the streets of Washington. Others watched on television.

There was a simple Mass for the Dead at St. Matthew's Cathedral. Jacqueline held the hands of John, Jr., and Caroline as they came out of the church and stood on the steps. According to custom, a riderless black horse, a sword dangling at its side and stirrups hanging backward from the saddle, trotted beside the caisson (a two-wheeled cart) with the body of the fallen leader. Six gray horses pulled the caisson. It was November 25, 1963, John, Jr.'s third birthday. The little boy gravely put his hand to his head and saluted the casket of his dead father.

Dignitaries from around the world attended John Kennedy's funeral. From left to right: President Heinrich Lübke of what was formerly West Germany; President Charles de Gaulle of France; Queen Frederika of Greece; King Baudouin of Belgium; Emperor Haile Selassie of Ethiopia; President Diosdado Macapagal of the Philippines; and President Park Chung Hee of South Korea.

Jacqueline Kennedy walked the mile or so from the cathedral to Arlington Cemetery, Robert Kennedy beside her. Many of those attending followed her. Cardinal Cushing gave the last blessing for the dead. Just as the cardinal finished his prayer, 50 jet fighter planes zoomed overhead. Troops on the ground presented arms. A 21-gun salute sounded. The strains of taps sounded over the grave. The flag that covered the casket was removed, folded, and placed in Jacqueline's hands.

For a moment Jacqueline's self-control threatened to break, but she regained her composure and stepped into the waiting limousine. She returned to the White House, where she received the international representatives who had attended the funeral and thanked them for coming.

An elderly man, top left, *uses his hat to salute his dead president.* At bottom left, *a woman wears a Kennedy campaign button reading,* "The Man for the 60s." *Holding commemorative programs, two women cry during a ceremony in New York,* top and bottom right.

◊ EPILOGUE ◊

Tributes to John Fitzgerald Kennedy, written and spoken, would fill volumes. Senator Mike Mansfield said, as he stood in the great Rotunda of the Capitol, "He gave us of a good heart, from which the laughter came. He gave us of a profound wit, from which a great leadership emerged. He gave us of a kindness and a strength fused into the human courage to seek peace without fear. . . ."

The sound of laughter was very much a part of the spirit of John Kennedy. There was a gaiety about him, a joy and zest for living that no amount of pain could subdue. The ability to laugh at himself was no small part of his charm. He took the world and its problems seriously—never himself.

A sense of urgency ran through all his actions, as though the tasks he had set himself could only be accomplished by ceaseless effort, and time was short. He was the first president to be born in the 20th century, and he was very much a man of his time. He was restless, seeking, with a thirst for knowledge, and he had a feeling of deep commitment, not only to the people of the United States, but to the peoples of the world.

To balance his idealism, he had the advantage of a logical mind. He had the ability to look at problems clearly and to focus the full power of his mind on their solutions.

Some critics have said that John Kennedy's presidency lacked "greatness." Still, many of the things he fought for— the rights of minorities, the poor, the very old and the very young, aid to education, better understanding among the peoples of the world—have come closer to being realized because of John Kennedy. It was he who set things in motion, he who moved the world in the direction of peace and cooperation. There was nothing small about John Kennedy. His dreams and hopes were big. His courage was monumental. His shadow still lies long across the land.

Representative Carl Elliot of Alabama said, "There was less hate about John Kennedy than any other person I have ever known. He met hate with compassion; he turned aside virulence with sparkling wit. . . ."

A student at the University of Arkansas wrote: "Youth identified themselves with him. They admired him because they understood his haste and boldness. They criticized him because they felt they were his peers, entitled to judge one of their own. And all the while they respected him, because they saw in him a leader who belonged to them, maybe even more than to the others."

At Marquette University in Wisconsin, a student wrote, "We begin to realize we must live in this world, and start to believe in something. No longer can we go on letting events pass by without realizing their significance. What kind of power is invested in mankind? Will we use our power as Lee H. Oswald did, or will we channel it in a direction that will preserve the human race, that will make one human proud to be part of the other?"

Perhaps E. B. White (author of the children's classic, *Charlotte's Web*), who received one of the first Freedom Awards from President Kennedy, sums him up best:

> When we think of him he is without a hat, standing in the wind and the weather. He was impatient of topcoats and hats, preferring to be exposed, and he was young enough and tough enough to confront and enjoy the cold and the winds of these times, whether the winds of nature or the winds of political circumstance and national danger. He died of exposure, but in a way that he would have settled for—in the line of duty, and with his friends and enemies all around, supporting him and shooting at him. It can be said of him, as of few men in a like position, that he did not fear the weather, and did not trim his sails, but instead challenged the wind itself, to improve its direction and to cause it to blow more softly and more kindly over the world and its people.*

*By permission of the author, E. B. White and *The New Yorker* magazine, where it appeared originally in the November 30, 1963 issue.

Appendix

Soon after the assassination, the Texas School Book Depository was swarming with police and Secret Service men. A 15-year-old boy had told a policeman that he'd seen something sticking out of a sixth-floor window as the presidential motorcade passed by. After a roll call of employees, only one person was missing—Lee Harvey Oswald, a shipping clerk. Oswald was a loner, a misfit, a discharged marine with communist leanings. A description and call were sent out to all police stations and radio receivers.

Later on the afternoon of November 22, 1963, Lee Harvey Oswald was arrested for the murder of John Kennedy. Although Oswald claimed he was innocent, evidence pointed to his guilt. But Oswald never had his day in court. As he was being transferred from a cell in the Dallas jail to a maximum security cell in the county jail, Jack Ruby, a Dallas dance-hall owner, shot Oswald. He died around 1:00 P.M. in the same hospital where President Kennedy had died the day before.

President Lyndon Johnson set up a fact-finding group under the direction of Chief Justice Earl Warren. After 10 months of investigation, the Warren Report said that Oswald was the only assassin of President Kennedy, but many people felt then and still feel that John Kennedy's assassination was the result of a conspiracy.

Jack Ruby was arrested and stood trial in Dallas. He was found guilty and was sentenced to hang. He died in jail, of cancer, on January 3, 1967.

Bibliography

Bill Adler, ed. *The Kennedy Wit*. New York: Citadel Press, 1964.

Binder, Otto O. *Victory in Space*. New York: Walker and Co., 1962.

Bishop, Jim. *A Day in the Life of President Kennedy*. New York: Random House, 1962.

Burns, James MacGregor. *John Kennedy, A Political Profile*. New York: Harcourt, Brace and Co., N.Y., 1959.

Caidin, Martin. *The Astronauts*. New York: E.P. Dutton and Co., 1962.

Collier, Peter, and David Horowitz. *The Kennedys: An American Drama*. New York: Simon and Schuster, 1984.

Donovan, Robert J. *PT 109*. New York: McGraw Hill, 1961.

Fuller, Helen. *Year of Trial*. New York: Harcourt Brace & World, 1962.

Heller, Deane and David. *Jacqueline Kennedy*. Derby, Conn.: Monarch Books, 1963.

Johnson, Haynes. *The Bay of Pigs*. New York: W.W. Norton, 1964.

Kennedy, John F. *Profiles in Courage*. New York: Harper and Row, 1956.

Kennedy, John F. *To Turn the Tide*, edited by John W. Gardner. New York: Harper and Bros., 1961.

Kennedy, Robert F. *Thirteen Days*. New York: Signet, New American Library, Inc., 1969.

Lee, Bruce. *A Boys' Life of J.F.K.* New York: Sterling, 1961.

Iris Luce, ed. *Letters from the Peace Corps*. Washington, D.C.: Robert B. Luce, Inc., 1964.

Lincoln, Evelyn. *My Twelve Years with John F. Kennedy*. New York: David McKay, 1965.

Lowe, Jacques. *Portrait: The Emergence of John F. Kennedy*. New York: McGraw Hill Book Co., 1961.

McCarthy, Joe. *The Remarkable Kennedys*. New York: Dial Press, 1961.

Manchester, William. *Portrait of a President*. Boston: Little, Brown, 1962.

Markmann, Charles L., and Mark Sherwin. *John F. Kennedy: A Sense of Purpose.* New York: St. Martin's Press, 1961.

Martin, Ralph G. *A Hero for Our Times.* New York: MacMillan, 1980.

Miers, Earl Schenck. *The Story of John F. Kennedy.* New York: Wonder Books, 1964.

Opotowsky, Stan. *The Kennedy Government.* New York: E.P. Dutton, 1961.

Schlesinger, Jr., Arthur M. *A Thousand Days.* New York: Houghton Mifflin, 1965.

Schoor, Gene. *Young John Kennedy.* New York: Harcourt Brace & World, 1963.

Seaborg, Glenn T. *Kennedy, Khrushchev, and the Test Ban Treaty.* Los Angeles: University of California Press, 1981.

Sorensen, Theodore. *Kennedy.* New York: Harper and Row, 1965.

Tanzer, Lester, ed. *The Kennedy Circle.* Washington, D.C.: Robert B. Luce, Inc., 1961.

U.S. Capitol Historical Society. *We, The People.* Washington, D.C.: U.S. Capitol Historical Society, 1964.

The Warren Commission. *The Warren Report.* New York: McGraw Hill, 1964.

The Warren Commission. *The Witnesses.* New York: McGraw Hill, 1965.

Whalen, Richard. *The Founding Father.* New York: NAL-World, 1964.

For Further Reading

Falkof, Lucille. *John F. Kennedy.* Ada, Oklahoma: Garrett Educational Corporation, 1988.

Kennedy, John F. *Why England Slept.* New York: Doubleday, 1961.

Randall, Marta. *John F. Kennedy.* New York: Chelsea House, 1988.

Schwarz, Urs. *John F. Kennedy.* London: Paul Hamlyn, 1964.

Selfridge, John W. *John F. Kennedy: Courage in Crisis.* New York: Fawcett Columbine, 1989.

White, Theodore H. *The Making of the President 1960.* New York: Atheneum, 1961.

INDEX

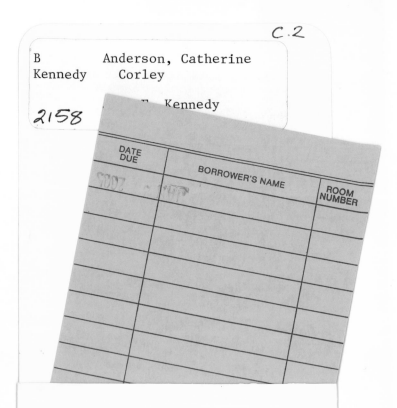

DATE DUE	BORROWER'S NAME	ROOM NUMBER
2005		

**The Glenelg Country School Library
Folly Quarter Road
Glenelg, Maryland   21737**